TRUE LIFE IN GOD

Vassula Rydén in Conversation with Jesus

Volume Eleven
Notebooks 95 - 101

ΙΧΘΥΣ   Edition

><del>—|></del>

Declaration

His Holiness Pope Paul VI has confirmed on 14 October, 1966, the decree of the Sacred Congregation for the propagation of the Faith, under number 58/16 (A.A.S.), permitting the publication of writings about supernatural apparitions, even if they do not have a 'nihil obstat' from ecclesiastical authorities.

In relation to Vassula Rydén, Cardinal Ratzinger stated (Guadalajara, Mexico 1996) "You may continue to promote her writings"; he requests only that one is discerning. He concluded by saying "Do not stifle the Spirit, do not despise prophesy, but test everything; hold on to what is good".

True Life in God

Vassula Rydén in Conversation with Jesus
Volume XI
(Typeset version of Notebooks 95 – 101 in original handwriting)

ΙΧθΥΣ

Published by:
English Association of True Life in God

First printing: March 2001 (United Kingdom)

Contents

The Eternal Father speaks to Vassula

Peace be with you; **My Command to you is**: go out where I send you to bear fruit that will last ♡ the Amen is with you; go round offering all that you have learnt from Me; **by the power of My Holy Spirit you shall walk, you shall talk, you shall move hearts, you shall cast out devils, you shall uproot evil and you shall plant goodness;** ... work faithfully in My Name, thrice Holy and carry out **My Command** ... stand your ground for this work of Mercy; resist evil and cling to Me; go, and do not be afraid to declare the truth; My Holy Spirit will remove all bounds to the truth; My Name: Peace and Love;

(March 18 1996)

Introduction

True Life in God:
A Transforming Experience

By: Archimandrite Eugene Pappas,
Greek Orthodox Church, NY, USA

Once in a long while an extraordinary event occurs that people mark in their minds and hearts, and date subsequent events from this marker. Such is the experience of an open heart reading "True Life In God" whose messages - I am convinced - are of Divinely inspired origin and are granted to us prophetically *(Acts 2:17)*, through Mrs. Vassula Rydén.

I will not belabor the point that these writings are scripturally intact and correct. Nor will I dwell on the fact that those who approach these messages with skepticism will remain skeptics. Nor will I try to explain why God has chosen Vassula to convey to us His word, once more. No "new" Good News (Ευαγγελιον) are being announced, yet, God's children hear the voice of their Father and know that it is He who speaks. He speaks to remind us of His eternal truths and to explain those things of His Word that have been ignored or miscalculated. The effects of His message and the impact of His words to His children are extraordinary. They are transforming. They are rejuvenating. This is what I want to talk about - albeit briefly - in this note.

I want to let everyone who reads this to know of a remarkable event. It is my experience that those that read and follow the messages of True Life In God behave as if they have been reborn into Christ! They have put on Christ as if to be enveloped by Him. They embrace their faith with a fire that is akin to that of the early neophyte Christians! They are even more attracted to their Church and follow Church Traditions and Sacramental Life with a rare devotion! From what I have observed, they live a life that is a *true life in God!*

What else could I as a pastor want from my flock of God? If these messages make them better Christians; if as a result of their reading of True Life In God they flock back into the Church and its Sacraments; if they not only understand their faith better, but are totally focused on living a Christ-like life; if they overflow with love for God and their neighbor; if they embrace an intimacy with God that resembles those of the Saints; if they submit their will to God and become examples for others; if the True Life In God messages cause such transformations, what more could I ask of my spiritual flock and congregation?

This transformation I have witnessed is without a doubt a "good fruit" of the Holy Spirit and hence the messages themselves must come from God *(Matt. 7:20).* I therefore will continue to study and draw from the Spirituality I have found in True Life In God.

New York
20 February, 2001

List of Headings to the
Messages in Notebooks 95 - 101

Headings are based on quotations from relevant Messages. Some longer Messages have more than one heading. The pages from which Vassula took the quotations are shown in brackets. The page numbers on which the actual Messages start are on the right.

Notebooks 95 – 101

12. 8. 1998

(After the 3 prayers said)

ah child!¹ child of the Father, of the Son and of the Holy Spirit! before you, I, Jesus, stand;² My delight and My garden in which I have built My heaven;³

because that day has approached on which all those that rebel against My Divinity are to be destroyed⁴ and stripped to the last of their auxiliaries; I am sending you in a country⁵ where you would stretch your shoots beyond the sea; I am sending you to a nation⁶ who resists all My Divine Calls of your times and who said in their night in a moment of folly: "we have to do something to shut the mouth of this woman;" I will send you there, My beloved, where My Heart continues to sob like a flute for them …. I will send you to them so that the olive tree once more produces its olive and the vine its fruit;⁷ ….

O watchman⁸ of the Tower! how much more will you gorge on your prey? but all your hateful menaces will go in vain … ⁹and you who burn incense to the Beast, how can you come to me entering My Sanctuary and presenting yourself in front of My

---

¹ *Jesus seemed very joyful*
² *I heard at the same time the word 'Am';*
³ *At the same time I heard the word 'Kingdom'*
⁴ *I also understood that it would be the "idea" that would be destroyed rather than the rebels themselves.*
⁵ *Italy*
⁶ *Rome, the 'Eternal City'.*
⁷ *Here there was a pause, as though Christ was reflecting, then His Voice raised like a Judge's …*
⁸ *Jesus was speaking to one particular person;*
⁹ *then to another one*

Throne saying: "I am safe and I am powerful to overturn any kingdom; I am safe to go on committing all these abominations; no one has seen me;"

I have; I have seen you and I will expose you to the nations …. look how you are falsifying by the lying pen of your tribe, My Law and My Institution of the Eucharist! can you still say: "Christ cannot see?" how is it that you who say, "I see", do not see or recognize your Saviour and your Inheritance? even the mole sees better than yourself and recognizes its hole;

come and repent, or are you incapable of repenting? let your eyes rain tears and repent; come and repent with all your heart and I will correct you gently and pardon you for all that you have done;

cease grieving My Holy Spirit; I hate pride and arrogance, but if you repent do not be afraid; see? your Redeemer is stretching out His Hand to you; the Holy One who gave you your priesthood and adorned you with royal vestments, investing you with emblems of authority to pasture His flock is telling you now as a father tells his son: "from the Beast's territory, My son, you inherit nothing, but from Me, your Lord, you will have everlasting life: I am your share and your inheritance;"

will I hear from you these blessed words: "I exult for joy in My Lord; my soul rejoices in My God thrice Holy, for He has clothed me in the garments of salvation, in His Divinity He has clothed me; and like a bridegroom who ornaments his bride, He has crowned me with a wreath that never withers; like a bride adorned in jewels I have been invested with His jewels; now let my God, in His Triune Glory, delight in me; let Spring[10] flower

---

[10] *here it means: 'God'.*

in my heart and in my bones; ah, how my soul rejoices in His Divinity which will be the emblem of my deification;

You who adorn every year the earth and revive its dryness, turning it into a bed of flowers of every hue, come and adorn my heart and turn it into a spring so that all the angels rejoice and say, 'look! he has Yahweh's Spring in him! the Bridegroom of all creation now can step in His garden, in His Paradise; the Lord of lords now can rejoice in him and gaze admiringly on His Own reflection; beauty and glory belong to the Most High; Garment of Glory,[11] do not delay to clothe your child in Royal Purple;'

graciously deign to hear me and deliver me from my ever so miserable flesh which was my empire that held me prisoner on this earth and its belongings; here, I am coming forward, in front of Your Throne to offer you my heart,[12] the only thing I own, as a token of my love; ah, adorable Bridegroom, transfigure my heart into a pure heart and deify me through the divine power of Your Holy Spirit, the Paraclete, the Divine; let Him shine within me like a Parousia now, and my soul will live and will glorify Your Triune Divinity as well;"

then I, Jesus Christ, will respond to you and say: "I will reward your humility by letting damnation eat herself up; she will be no more your dark companion, for you have now replaced evil with love, exchanged darkness with light; and although you will continue to live in your flesh, your spirit will be walking in heaven and your heart that you have given Me will have its wedding; yes, My child, for as the bridegroom rejoices in his bride, so will your God and All rejoice in you; Boundless Goodness will be your kin from now on;"

---

[11] *The angels exclaimed to God: "Garment of Glory", because someone who is in a state of holiness can be said that he is clothed with Christ.*
[12] *Free will too.*

…. and you, My Vassula, I tell you: at the favourable time I will send you to them and you will show yourself; I discharge you now, My delight, so that you attend your other duties as well;[13]

I wish I could have been like Mary
and not like Martha;
I am happy when I sit with
You, adorable One,
enjoying and feasting in Your Presence;

do not complain, Vassula, enjoy yourself in Me; listen, will it console you were I to tell you how in this ineffable Love I have for you, I have you embedded as an emerald in My royal crown? would it console you, My Own, were I to tell you that you are My wreath of perfumed flowers that never wither since they adorn My Head, and that you are to Me like a concert of sweet music in My Ears? would it console you were I to tell you that you have become My spiritual throne and that My visitations to you are like a scent of delicate perfumes given to Me?

a generous heart is what the Lord needs; there have been so many moments in which My Eyes were turned on you alone and for you alone; ah, Vassula!

ah, my Lord   Most High!
my eyes are fixed on You;
my whole mind and heart as well ….
You have truly captured my heart in
Your Divine Love and in
Your royal munificence;

---

[13] *Housework of course ….*

4

and you Mine;

You are my only delight!

and you, My Vassula, you are My only delight when your eyes look fervently, with ardour and with love for Me .... to have Me in your heart is Life;

Life is You ....

My Work,[14] hide in Me and rejoice in Me, so enter into the delights of your Saviour; I, the Lord, will reveal more of My Heart to you;

come; I bless you;

$$ΙΧΘΥΣ \quad \rightleftharpoons$$

29. 8. 1998

Lord, Gracious One,
Come to me!
The bonds of death were all round me,
but You have stepped out of
heaven in Your Glorious manner
and with Splendour,
and in Your royal munificence
liberated me;

---

[14] *We are all the Work of His creation, but it means here also, the transfiguration the Lord made out of me: my conversion.*

I had hands but they could not feel,
feet, that did not walk,
a heart, that did not beat,
and no sound
ever came from my throat to praise You;
Yet, in Your faithful Love, Lover of mankind,
Bridegroom of Your creation,
You leaned all the way
from the heights towards me, the unworthy one,
to revive me, and to transform me into a song
for You and Your House;

Behold, what You have done to a sinner,
without You thinking twice that You might
be risking to cheapen Your Works;
You have clothed Yourself in me[15]
so that You may parade me in Your Courts;
and with great glee You taught me Your precepts;
You taught me that Integrity should be used as my rod
fighting on Your side;

In Your Goodness You made me penetrate
into Your motives to be able to understand Your methods;
You have grafted me on Your Heart, a gesture of espousals
so that You and I take pleasure in Your Divine Love;

You taught me to enter into Your Joy
and to love You so that when I speak of You,
I would speak of Your awesome Power,
recounting Your Greatness and Your munificence;

ah, Vassula, sing to Me and be My harp as well;

---

[16] *It means "I am clothed with Christ"*

in My Love, I have given you life; watching over, in My care, every breath you took; My Word is Life; can anybody say:

"God has not acted;"

in the light of grace I have veiled you, to be Mine and in ceaseless contemplation on My Heart;

unlike others who receive My Word as a gift and whom I visit when I wish, I have given you a unique gift, this one of calling Me at any time you wish;

see? I have given you this special privilege in proportion to the task I have entrusted you with, and in proportion to My burden on you;

see, how I measured everything when I planned this? not that you were qualified in yourself for this most noble task of reviving and uniting My House; all your qualifications come from My bounty, they come from Me; I have made you the vessel that carries this immense treasure, frail, but clear, that such an overwhelming Power does not come from you but from Me, your God; I am dwelling in you, this is why there is no weakening on your part;

have I not the right to use you, serving as a reminder of My Mercy for the rest of you?

You invited me to Your Banquet ...

I have invited you to My Banquet and through you many others ....

I am bound by the vows I have made
to You and I want to pay You the
debt of thanks and work faithfully
for Your House; for You have
not only saved my life from death
but You have allowed me in
Your folly of Love to walk freely in
Your Presence any time and in any hour
of the day bathing me in Your Light;

You have bound me with bonds of
Love and Friendship, pressing me on
Your Sacred Heart so that no mortal
can distract this divine union any more;

In Your exuberant Love,
You made me strong like a tower
towards those who storm over me;
terror assails them in broad daylight
at the sound of Your Holy Spirit,
my Companion and my Joy ....

My pillar, supporting My Cross of Unity, radiate the light of the Knowledge of My Glory, radiate in this darkness, the light of My munificence and do not fear; I have poured anointed oil in your mouth so that you may speak for Me; be My chantress, always of good cheer; sing to this generation by travelling round the world, relying on My grace;

let all those who by grace were called to read this Hymn of Love and led to taste this hidden manna, prosper, while still in their exile;

I grant to all those who have been called to read My Love Hymn with a contrite heart, sanctifying graces; may their hearts contemplate the glory of My Magnificence and My fatherly Love and see in Me not only an Almighty God, but also a God of Goodness, most loving and an intimate Friend; may their ears hear the sighs and groanings of My Heart and be reassured of My Clemency;

I have set a guard[16] at your side, a watcher at the gate of your heart to watch that no intruder diverts you from your mission;

when you speak, My love, keep always to the point; yes, repeat all My sayings but in few words; set the jewels I have given you in each heart;

let everyone know that My Conversations are sweetness itself;

I am with you;   **ic**

1. 10. 1998

Open my ear, O Lord,
awaken me from my sleep,
thrust Your Mighty Hand
from heaven and lift me!

ah Vassula, all heaven rejoices when from a mere creature a sound is heard in Our Celestial Courts ....

---

[16] *I understood, a special angel.*

from dross I have turned you into silver, and from silver into the most exquisite of jewels; My child, let your eyes be fixed ahead; be like a graceful garland for My Head and fill My Heart with joy by enduring the hardships in silence for My sake;

men will often attack you, but they will never overcome you; your labours for My sake will never go in vain, but will yield fields of instruction, prospering generations;

May my tongue recite your Love Hymn,

May my lips proclaim Your Righteousness and Your great deeds of Love;

My favour is upon you and you have My blessings;

ah, My child, words of hate fly all around Me, though I give no cause for hostility;[17] in return for My faithfulness they denounce Me;

But who withstood the might of Your Arm?

no one .... no one withstood the might of My Arm; have I not shown My strength when people abused Me? I am known to confound the haughty by My absolute power; pray for the one[18] who breathed out fire on his soul ...

---

[17] *I understood that Jesus meant that His words in me can create hostility towards the hardened hearts.*
[18] *In Rhodos, Greece, the Orthodox Vicar after finding out that a young Jewish man after reading "True Life in God" had asked to be baptised and join the Greek Orthodox Church, refused to give him the permission.*
We sent a lawyer friend of ours to plead with the Vicar, but the Vicar's heart hardened even more, and said: "I shall not give the permission for baptism even if this matter causes me to go to hell." This is why Jesus asks us to pray for the Vicar's soul which he threw away in his folly.

may this nation[19] I so loved prosper in righteousness; remain in My Love and keep My Commandments; I am the Way the Truth and the Life; listen Israel, He who scattered you is gathering you and I will be guarding you Israel[20] like the pupil of My Eye;

so dear a son to Me, Israel, you have indeed accepted Me by the power of My Holy Spirit, may you prosper in My Divinity and in My Love; love Me as I love you; I tell you: I shall draw all people to Myself for in Me are Eternal Life and Glory; be one in My Name and follow Me in My Blood-stained foot-prints ♡ **ic**

Vassula, I, Jesus, am with you; your Maker and Redeemer who formed you is with you and on your side ♡ allow Me to engrave on you the rest of My Love Hymn; rest in Me and I will rest in you so loved one;

I, Jesus, bless you; **ic**

15. 10. 1998

*Lord, give words to my ear and
apply my heart to know them;
yes, because Your Word,
Lord of Compassion, is my delight,
my joy, the knowledge of the sages;
have Your Word always ready on my lips;
fill my mouth with nothing else
than this Celestial Manna;*

---

[19] *Israel, but also all those Jews who discover the Truth and get baptized, and there are many.*
[20] *for the newly baptized ones into Christianity*

ah Vassula, have I not written for you hundreds of pages of instruction and knowledge for you to be able to expound the Truth and with sound words to answer those who question you? I am righteous in all that My Hand undertakes; concentrate now upon Me for My glory, and do not let your mind dictate to you; let nothing come between you and Me;[21] have I not, in My divine munificence adorned your soul wherein I dwell? have you not seen the fruits of My graces?

My beloved, let the treasure I have entrusted you with be the salvation to many souls; by My Divine authority I have called you and commissioned you, in spite of your failings, to restore My House and My honour;

if it[22] were not genuine would your soul, as well as of others be drawn to praise Me and long for lengthy contemplation on My Divinity, speaking graciously on My Perpetual Presence?

have I not clothed Myself in you, even in visible form?[23] and who, tell Me, reconciled you to the Father, showing you and through you the splendour and true image of the Father? and who instructed you that We[24] are the Bridegroom of our creation?

the signs of My Graciousness I have shown you are many; be reassured, My beloved, that I have indeed called you at My royal banquet;

---

[21] *A mere dark thought transgressed my mind: 'what if I was wrong?' I wanted to be reassured.*
[22] *This revelation*
[23] *The Lord means, when people have seen Him on me, and my face disappeared.*
[24] *the Trinity*

when the Bridegroom leads His bride into privacy to converse intimately and hold her on His Heart, bending towards her, after the Feast, would she object? .... would **you** object? so be active when I want you active and among crowds, but now pass your time with Me in a holy contemplation resting in Me, abandoning yourself to My good pleasure; do not think that you will be less fruitful; come enter into the Divine joy of your Saviour;

(Our Lord's loving words reassured me;)

remember, My beloved, that true and pure theology is the contemplation of Me, your God and Lover of mankind;

be blessed;

ΙΧθΥΣ ⤳

19. 10. 1998

Lord, help me in all,
help me to make atonement
for Your people, for Your Church,
to offer sacrifice, prayers,
that would rise like incense in heaven,
and would be as an appeasing fragrance,
for the Father, a holy oil for the Son,
and a consecration to the Holy Spirit;

O Holy Trinity, embroidery of my soul,
superb ornamentation of my heart,
emblem of my mind,
chime of my voice, sentinel of my being,
what could I say much more and still fall short?

alone[25] We encircled Our territory, in Our one Substance and one Power and one Knowledge We are one God alone, yes, with one Will and one Dominion, We encircled Our property,[26] to give it a disciple's tongue, anointing Our Divine Work;[27]

in Our Power We poured Ourselves in you like a vivifying liquid; like the sun shining in spring We shone on you, fortifying Our city and sanctuary[28] before your oppressors would ill-treat you;

in Our Knowledge We appeared to you, communicating Ourselves to you, instructing you and through you, others, with the knowledge the sages have received;

feast[29] of Our Mercy! enjoyment of Our Trinitarian Holiness, be rooted in Our Will and be like a sprig of frankincense in summertime, to continue to manifest the Truth and give a better explanation of the Revelation given to you;

We will flood you with Our Light for a better understanding of Our Word, imprinting Our Divine Image in every word given to you; Our Majesty will supply all you still lack; 'then like an olive tree loaded with fruit, like a vessel of beaten gold encrusted with every kind of precious stone'[30] you will atone with dignity in this hour of painful apostasy, and like cantors chanting hymns of praise, your frail voice will plead with Us with Our terms, with Our understanding and within Our Will; in Our royal munificense We have in Our embracement endowed your heart

---

[25] *by Their Free Will the Holy and most Divine Trinity made me their Own and came to dwell in me, for They Decided, and no one else*
[26] *me*
[27] *my being created*
[28] *We are the City & Sanctuary of God who dwells in us.*
[29] *God called out to me: Feast!*
[30] *Si 50 : 10 + 9*

with Wisdom so that It can be passed on to this generation and that they may profit from It;

so, little one, continue to walk in the path laid out with sapphires for you, and be a herald and apostle of Our Trinitarian Deity; seed every country so that Our Kingdom stretches from sea to sea; mountains and hills shall bow low at Our saving justice; and, in Our Power, We shall call into existence those things that are not,[31] as those that are;[32]

I am the Life and the Resurrection who brings the dead to life; remain devout to Me and blossom; never fret; be like the rose that grows on the bank of a watercourse; be blessed and give off to your Saviour a sweet smell like incense, spreading your fragrance together with Mine in My House, inebriating My household into conversion and into one heart;

I will protect you from fury and jealousy; say: "all the Works of the Lord are good and He will supply every want in due time;"[33] yes, praise My Works and be My Paradise in this way, Paraskevi 'μου';[34]

O Lord, let me keep Your Instructions
in mind and do not allow forgetfulness
take the better of Me!

Steady my feet, Glorious Lord,
and keep me awake and at Your Service ...

---

[31] *bring to a spiritual Resurrection this generation*
[32] *then, Jesus spoke alone.*
[33] *Si 39:33*
[34] *In Greek: 'μου' = "my", Paraskevi*

My child, Wisdom illumined in your soul, like a sweet flame, ceaselessly revealing to you Our secrets, but also Ourselves in such a way that it may revive this generation, invigorating it to grow into Our splendour and become worthy to enter Paradise;

by Our Own free-Will, We, in Our Triune Glory, it so pleased Us to befriend you intimately and pour on you in abundance torrents of delights and consolations; We revealed to you something forgotten by My Church: this overflowing sweetness, yes! Almighty God's divine sweetness that attracts myriads of angels around My Throne, countless souls to worship Me and delight in this heavenly banquet; in Our ineffable sweetness We embrace all Heaven;

My Church has forgotten, yes, and neglected Me, My Own Spouse .... She remains naked, and shows no interest in My Divine sweetness; "how is it, My Bride, you turn your back to Me when I open My Heart to you to converse with you? My Heart is filled with ineffable sweetness, ah, but you have not understood what draws My creation to Me ...."

My intimate companion, avert your eyes from your surrounding, and fix your eyes, your mind and your soul in a holy contemplation on My Heart, and allow Me to continue our sweet and intimate converse with you;

a life spent generously for Me by your own free will infatuates Me, your Divine Companion; a life which suffered insult and calumny for My Sake affects Me to tears; joy-of-My-Heart, you have still not quite understood how, in My fervent love I have for you, I joined Myself inseparably with you so you become one spirit with Me; so remain in My Peace; My faithful Love will never leave you;

> *ah, my King, my heart is stirred*
> *by Your noble theme,*
> *inebriated when You address me;*
> *Gracefulness[35] is upon me like dew,*
> *shadowing me in His mighty embrace,*
> *my stronghold is God Himself*
> *the God who loves me faithfully;*

you see, My love, every structure knit together in Me, grows into holiness and purity in My Divinity; therefore, you, My Vassula, in Me, are being built up into a holy vessel where I am contained, a pure and holy dwelling-place for Our Triune Holiness, in the Spirit, in which We could contemplate Ourselves; so rejoice and be glad before your Bridegroom who is ever so generous to you; remain blameless and I shall never fail you;

now, joy-of-My-Heart, you may return to your other duties; receive from your Saviour His Kiss of Divine Love on your forehead;

I, Jesus Christ, bless you;   **ic**

20. 10. 1998

> *My Lord and my God,*
> *You are truly most Beautiful,*
> *and immersed in Your Beauty*
> *You are Divine and Pure;*
> *how am I and all the others*
> *not to fall in love with Your Sweetness?*

---

[35] *God*

Gracefulness is a dew upon Your Lips,
and in Your majesty and splendour
You have blessed us, courted us, favoured us
and covered us with inumerable gifts,
not only to resemble Your angels,
but to resemble You;

Your Word is like a brocade
which You have clothed me with,
adorning my soul for Your majesty;
and all of this You have done with the
greatest delight, and with no thought
that You might have been cheapening
Your Sceptre of Your kingship!

God has annointed me ....

indeed I have and with great joy that is ....

come now and lean on Me; more loyal than Myself you will not find; stronger and more powerful than Myself you will not find; I am the Rock and the Foundation of Christianity; I am He who is, was and is to come;

partners we have become; I and you, you and I, knit together in one; no human strength could have raised your soul except if it were given from above;

in all truth I tell you: your Bridegroom will continue to drench you by the dew of heaven,[36] so that you too in your turn will drench the arid soil with torrents of Instruction; then the fig tree will produce its figs and the vine its grapes; the olive crop will

---

[36] *I understood also: by the graceful Presence of Jesus Christ.*

enrich, for the time has come for My Divine Justice to topple the wicked who prostrate in front of the Beast;

soon the storm will be over ….

- serve My House and speak in My Name so that I, in My transcendent Love, may continue to pour My blessings on this generation;

- serve My House and make My Name thrice Holy sound like music to the apostatized ears and they will be healed;

- serve my House without reserve, My chosen one, with My pure Manna and fill the starved mouths with My Word;

- serve My House so that It recovers its vigour by reminding It that My Presence lights up any darkness;

ah, Vassula, tell them how I am waiting for them to invite Me, and as soon as I will see their lips parted, ready to pronounce the first words of invitation, I will come down to them and lift them from those murky waters to soar with Me on the wings of the wind; I will not conceal Myself nor My Joy but I will speak to them in poetry, unfolding the mysteries one after the other;

on the dry soil I will pour out water,[37] and streams[38] on the arid ground; I will pour out My Spirit as well as My Blessings and everyone will spring up; sated with the dew of heaven in their spirit they will honour Me;

---

[37] *Blessings*
[38] *Holy Spirit*

your tender Bridegroom affirms these things to you again; those things that I, in My triune holiness revealed to you long ago; there is no Rock but I, your God;

see the wonderful deeds I am doing for My House? I instituted you as a witness in My House and I have established My Work everywhere I wanted It to be;

see how I love My House? girded with power, I Am; so raise your voice in My House and ask My shepherds: "is there anyone willing to work with vigour and love to rebuild this tottering House? is there anyone in there who is willing to defend this House? is there anyone who understands now what I am saying? is there anyone in the Lord's House who is disposed to expand the Kingdom of God?"

if there is anyone willing, I then, will shine on him with My splendour, clothing him with Myself; I shall make Myself known to him and he will see Me standing before him; he will see the Eternal and Immortal King, and he will draw all men to Me because I would have enriched his soul with My immutable Divinity, and would have adorned him with every ornament imaginable, and in his royal stature he would heal this generation; the deaf will hear and the blind will see and all together in one voice will cry out: "we belong to the Holy Trinity: the Father, the Son and the Holy Spirit";

and you, Vassula, weary not of writing; bring forth abundant fruit; all My angels rejoice at the sight of these fruits;

I am on your side, so do not fear;

I love you; **ic**

20

5. 11. 1998

(In the U.S.A. much controversy was being exercised on me, before my coming; it seemed, as once our Lord told me, that at the approach of the Holy Spirit all the demons go wild, and the demon puts all his power of evil forces to create chaos. What a typical way of the devil to combat the safvific message of Our Saviour! and how many times has he exercised it before my arrival on those who are God's devout children! May these souls who allow Satan to whisper in their ears and listen to him, be forgiven, and preserved from harm .... Nevertheless, since all of this noise issued from the depths of Hell, the Mighty Hand of God was able to chase it away, and our Lord triumphed in the end; thousands came, assembling to hear our Lord's message, and those who were victims of Satan giving false statements on heresay to prevent me from being present, were left powerless ...)

Blessed is he who cares for justice and acts with integrity ...

My child, learn that every tongue that prophesied accusations on you, in Judgement will be refuted unless they repent; prayer and expiating incense is what they need;

at the sound of My Holy Spirit all the demons are tormented and reinforce their strength in every way, going to extremes, assailing My mouthpieces by merciless anger and falsehood, for those Dominations, Principalities and Powers have great force upon the earth, but do not fear, they are submissive to My commands; they recoil before Me and tremble before My Cross;

with oil I have anointed you, My merry messenger, to be My Echo of Love, of Unity and Reconciliation; I am saying again and again that I have made you a witness to My people, see? all are assembling and coming to hear My Love Hymn and when they do, they grow radiant because I, like a sun, shine on them My brightness and My Glory;

today I tell you: your Saviour will bring His victory nearer; My Return will not be late; I will bring salvation to those who love Me;

from the beginning I foretold the future and predicted beforehand events to come, but many people's hairs have turned grey already and **still** they have not understood My sayings and never will; hence, I will grant you an understanding; **I** had warned you once,[39] generation, that because of this Great Apostasy, the rebels[40] who call themselves scholars by grade, stormed secretly a passage into My Sanctuary to pillage and plunder freely with the intention to stamp down like the mud in the streets, My Divinity and My Perpetual Sacrifice, establishing legislators of infamous laws;

I have said that My Hand is still raised to strike and that My Justice will blow on you, arousing limitless blisters upon you, scorching your generation and every living thing around it; many then would want to breathe but would only inhale a scorching wind, that would burn them inwardly leaving them as a living torch;

did you not know, degenerate generation, that in these days of darkness you are living in, you have been inhaling a **scorching apostasy**? an apostasy burning you inwardly and outwardly, producing limitless blisters in your inmost being? some would ask, "why has God done this to us?" have you not read: "the

---

[39] *On the 3.7.88*
[40] *In other words, the rebels represent "the smoke of Satan", predicted by the Pope Paul VI.*

anger of God is being revealed in your times, from heaven against all the impiety and depravity of men **who keep truth imprisoned** in their wickedness;"[41] but there is not one who understood My sayings ....

I had been asking for great and truthful expiations, so that you would not have to suffer the consequences of this Apostasy, but I have received very few expiations because My sayings were censored for lack of trust in Me; they did not trust Me and did not believe in My Power entirely, to spread My sayings and warn this generation;

your own behaviour, generation, and actions have brought this Apostasy on you, and it pierces your heart, but at the same time too while I am saying this to you, My Eyes fill with Tears of Blood, and My Heart continues to sob like a flute for all of you ....

today you call out, generation: "my God, I am in anguish for my family and for myself; I writhe with pain from this burning wind;" but to this day My sayings are ignored and are not taken seriously; you gasp for fresh air, while you are burning inwardly, and yet, when My Holy Spirit of Grace descends in power upon you to set you free and comes in glory to you so that you inhale the Breath of Life, the Breath of God, that is the Holy Spirit, your rebellious and unruly hearts continue to reject Me;

My Return is imminent but nor that have you fully grasped its meaning; and so it is, My Vassula, My Love for all of you compels Me to bring foreward My Return;

---

[41] *Rm 1 : 18*

Almighty Power, Wisdom and Goodness will prevail before not long; ecclessia will revive in its Triune Glory; blessed is he who allows Me to reside in his soul;

blessed is he who leans on My Bosom and allows Me to embrace him

Notebook 96

his soul will be recognized[42] in My Courts from the odour of My fragrance upon him;

blessed is he who receives My Word and keeps it, he would be adjudged holy;

tell this generation and especially those who do not know Me that I, in My Divine Love, who have given you mystical graces to raise the Church, embellish it and give Her Sources of Living Water, am the Author of this revelation and am holding back the even greater graces of My Power, for these will be given to you later on and in due course;

You have given me freely
from Your Own Goods;
Lord, Lover of Life,
Your gift of Mercy
has saved me and many others;

Glory be to God,
praised be His Holy Name;

---

[42] *accepted*

rest now, My Beloved in your Resting Place,[43] the tuneful heartbeats you hear are My Sighs of Love for each one of you;

come, we, us?

ΙΧΘΥΣ ⟩○─▷

11. 11. 1998

My Lord, most gracious,
I beg You to come and cultivate my will
that it becomes Your Will,
stripping it and transforming it to be nothing else
but Your Divine Will;
come and kill everything in me that offends You
so that by this clement gesture of Yours,
in the day of Judgment
You would find me faultless and
agreeable in Your sight;

Jesus, because You have died out of Your
exuberant love for me, to give me life and happiness
and be able to share Your Kingdom and Your glory,
mark me as Yours for eternity;

My priest,[44] continue to place garlands of love on My Head; replace My thorned Crown that this generation forces joyfully on My Head and continues to drag Me by force into new Gethsemanes; I have, in My exhuberant love, but as well as in

---

[43] *His Sacred Heart;*
[44] *1 P 2 : 9*

My agonies similar to those of Gethsemane, written all these pages to all of you so that you believe in the power of My Holy Spirit who bears witness; reverence Me in your heart, Paraskevi, by giving Me your time to write down again My words filled with sighs and sorrows; never cease praying and keep your mind focused only on My immutable Divinity;[45]

ah, My child …. continue to be patient and out of your patience I will keep flowing into dry lands, immersing them in My Divine Love with heavenly dew, giving growth where dross is still to be found; do not allow your heart to be troubled, trust in Me, your Creator, for I can do great things; I am infinitely rich in grace and virtue, therefore, I invite you, My bride, to share with your Bridegroom the glorious Instrument of our espousals, that is, the splendour of My Cross ….

(I understood that this invitation of sharing the Cross was an invitation not only to share It but as well as to fully penetrate into the mystery of our Lord's Passion, for this invitation was already offered to me in the very beginning of my call; our Lord, our Spouse, the Lover of mankind was stepping out, once more, of His Throne to give me a fuller knowledge of the worth (value) of the Cross;)

come willingly as you do every time I call you into My embrace …[46] to embrace Me is to embrace My Cross …. and now let Me breathe in you My Divine Words:

I have said to you that when you embrace Me you are embracing My Cross and in this embrace you are bathed in My Light; the way, and I would say again, the **only** way to a union of Divine

---

[45] *Jesus then gave a long sigh.*
[46] *There was a slight pause then with a change of tone of voice that became very grave He said: "to embrace Me is to embrace My Cross …."*

Love with Me is when you voluntarily embrace with love My Cross which you know bears its sufferings but its joys as well and which would lead you where your soul will be exalted: to Calvary ♡

in My sweet embrace you will find joys but the greatest joy of all is when you discover that you became a copy of My Passion, and part of Me, the Supreme Victim: another sacrifice of love, another living crucifix, another slave to be sold to the whole world; and being in My embrace your soul will be drawing from Me strength and all the virtues to resemble Me;

enamoured of My Spirit, your heart will chant hymns of praise reaching the heights and to the Amen's ears and so your Triune God will be glorified ....

who in your days understands fully the splendour of My Cross? very few do; this is why I come through you to instruct with passion, the world; in My thirst for souls and in My agony seeing them fall in the eternal fires, I call every one in this world for conversion and to prepare you for My glorious Reign of the Kingdom on earth, in which My Divine Will becomes the essence of your daily life and the emblem on your forehead;

I call out in the night of your souls, peering now and then through the window of your heart hoping to hear these words from you: "come, Beloved Saviour, come and open the eyes of my Night, and turn my heart to Your Goodness and away from evil; come and open the gates of Virtue to me so that I come in and prostrate in reverance before your Triune Glory; Beloved of my soul, give me once more, life, by Your Glorious Word;" and I will answer you: "I will never fail you, in honour of My Name, I, who transcend earth and heaven in majesty, will grant you Life;"

satisfy Me now, Vassula, by leaning on Me; rest Me in your heart willingly, dedicating your time for Me; love the Unloved and follow My instructions;

I, Jesus, bless you, telling you: My heaven is in you;

tomorrow I will continue My Message; **ic**

(The following day, Christ returned and called me for dictation and so my heart in joy, welcomed Him with these words):

> *In Your exuberent love, Lord of Mercy,*
> *in Your divine tenderness come to my side;*
> *Your branded slave is at Your service;*

you have been honoured to be branded, marking you as My belonging, as My possession .... these marks are noble and priceless and I reveal them to those to whom I wish to reveal them, even though they are not seen by the exteriour eye, they are seen, by grace, with the eye of the soul;[47]

I, Myself, came into the world to serve and not to be served; I had, although My state was Divine, emptied Myself to assume the condition of a slave; since My Father gave Me to all of you as a gift for your redemption with My entire Will too,[48] I, in My turn, in your days, call for My purpose, My Chosen ones and lift them for My Salvific Plan, turning them into copies of Myself;

---

[47] *As our Lord says that only by grace a soul is favoured to be able to perceive with the 'eye of the soul' things that are not exteriour and visible by the normal eye; even the marks of His Passion, branding a soul, (interiour marks,) can be given to a soul who would feel them, thus becoming a copy of the Supreme Victim.*

[48] *Jesus' Will was the same as His Father's Will;*

chosen long before their creation with the intention to become the true image of Myself and co-operators of My Love Plan, I honour them to be branded with the same marks I Myself had been branded with to make them fully Mine and to show the world that they are truly Mine and that they are My seed .... so when these are exposed to persecution, spittle, and are threatened, when they are misunderstood, calumniated and attacked, know that they come from Me and that they are the bone of My bone, the flesh of My flesh;

branded with all these noble signs that I received for your redemption, these noble souls too, for your sake, impious generation, are being tread upon, massacred daily and brought to judgement even by the dignitaries of My Church! just as sheep brought for the slaughter, they too are led by the false accusations of those who contribute to this day, the slaughter of My saints and My prophets of all times, **and how ingeniously they get round My words[49] in order to justify their incredulity!**

their[50] conduct does not please Me because they become the enemies of the whole human race, since they are hindering My Chosen ones from pronouncing My Will to My people and from reconstructing My House; thus, these oppressors, are reaching all the time the full extent of their iniquity;

as I have said, My Vassula, I am giving you to all the nations as My gift, that is: for their own benefit, to echo My Words and to serve the Church;

I intended you from all eternity to become a true image of Myself, sharing My sufferings so that one day you will share My

---

[49] *Jesus means that these people do not use the words of counsel of Jesus: "You will know them by their fruits;"*
[50] *1 Th. 2 : 15 – 16*

Glory; in the Light of My Cross model yourself with My Mind; working for the Light that is the same as to work for the exaltation of My Cross;

I have, My beloved one, given you a spirit of perseverance to keep up with My pace; the night is almost over and it will be daylight soon – so courage, daughter, courage …. in your union with My Cross you have done all these things in My Name, that is you have witnessed, in My Name, My Messages to the utmost of your capacity; this has been done to fulfil the text: "those who have never heard or seen Me will hear Me and see Me and those that never understood Me will understand Me by the grace of My Holy Spirit;"

therefore, continue to embrace My Cross, stretching further than the seas with My Love Hymn in one hand and My Cross in the other; be My cheerful messenger, never abandoning My Cross; keep pronouncing My Will and all these things that you have heard and learnt from Me and be My joy and My heaven;

remember: I have offered you to share My Unity Cross with Me and you are to remain grafted on your Divine Bridegroom between His Bosom and on to My Cross; let your eyes perceive through My Cross those things that are invisible but eternal and not those things that are visible and wear away one day; so look through My Cross for the things that It can offer you later on in heaven;

all the Riches that can be found in My Heart could be seen through the Eye of your Redemptive Instrument and of your salvation: My Cross …. the proof that any one is joined and one with Me, formed in Me and knit with Me is when your heart is grafted as well on My Cross with all its bearings; anybody who is convinced that he belongs to Me must understand that he belongs to My Cross as well;

have you not read: [51] "to suffer in God's way means changing for the better[52] and leaves no regrets, but to suffer as the world knows suffering brings death; just look what suffering in God's way has brought you – what keenness, what explanations, what indignation and what alarm; what yearning," and I would add to this, what joy, what intense perseverance and fortitude;

having then been brought by grace to distress,[53] so that you repent, the eyes of your soul opened because you diligently obeyed My Voice; My Vassula, look at how I have led you to repentance, look at how I have led you to My Cross; look at the joy I have obtained when you voluntarily thrust yourself to Me, then to My Cross!

My joy is overflowing and I am filled with consolation; gathering My lambs is not an easy task let alone uniting them, daughter, but giving Me your confidence in these matters, trust, love and faith, I can advance in you, spreading My Message as I want it spread, and, My Vassula, through your trials I triumph;

be in peace and continue to live in the Light of My Cross: a true life in Me,

Jesus Christ;

ΙΧΘΥΣ 

---

[51] *2 Co: 7 : 10 - 11*
[52] *Yes, because it leads to repentance then to the embracement of the Cross.*
[53] *back in 1985*

28. 11. 1998

*Today it is 13 years of anointed messages; I've been in
meditation all day long; meditation on how all this unmerited
grace was given me; I was saying:*

*"no one has found
so much favour in God's Eyes
in the wretched condition I was found;*

*God has had great mercy on my soul;
the King of Kings brought me into
His Royal Household;*

*He summoned me by my name,
and invited me at His great banquet,
treated me with royal prodigality;
then as though all of this
did not seem to appease
His eagerness of satisfying me,
out of His excessive and
exuberent love He has for me,
the King of Kings gave
me privileged access at any time to
His Royal Presence;
to walk in and out of
His Royal Courts freely;*

*my wretchedness, and it seemed
my nothingness had won His favour;*

in His determination to save me
He revealed to me
heaven and earth and
all the marvels that are under heaven;

and so to praise His Holy Name,
our Lord and God,
taught me how to hymn His Name;"

O Lord, although Death was
staring me in the face,
Your great Power saved me;
You yielded Your Royal Sceptre
to what did not exist;[54]

may every one commemorate the
Power of Your Name and
Sceptre for evermore;
You have, with joy, displayed
to my miserable soul,
Your Riches and unending
splendours of Your Kingdom;
You have never dealt with me
as my faults deserved
but You had given orders to my angel saying:

"take her; bring her home safe and sound
to Us[55] *and to our House ..."*
and so he did ...

---

[54] *Figurative meaning: 'I did not exist, until our Lord resurrected me from my Spiritual death.'*
[55] *The Trinity*

- (After this, my angel drew my attention; I asked him, like in the old times to draw me something ....)

daughter – of – the – Most – High,
peace, peace, enter into the joy of our Lord;
be obedient to Him, alone,
I, your guardian angel,
offer you this rose from My heart;
understand and learn to know our Lord;
enter into the Sacred Heart;
God has called you and now you have made peace with God;

I, Daniel, servant of God, carried you to the Most High;
heaven today is rejoicing;
come, approach with confidence the Throne of Grace;

I, Daniel, bless you, in the Most Holy Trinity;

Daniel – Servant – of - God;

(the Father, leaned from Heaven and approached me ....)

My Vassula, nothing pleases Me more than when you gather yourself in My Presence; extol My Word; I, God, am looking down from heaven, into your room, flower; you have seen My Glory, you have tasted My sweetness and you have obtained My favour; before the mountains were born, before anything on earth had sprout, I had chosen you, My loved one, to sing a melodious tune honouring My Name thrice Holy and giving life with My Word to the dead; I had, My child, since your birth put you in My Angel's charge to guard you and carry you to Me; see? can any one say: "God has not displayed His Divine Power; God has not been mindful of His Love and Faithfulness to His creation;"

ah, Vassula, it has been thirteen perfumed years, thirteen years of anointed Messages confided to you so that you pronounce, to nations, My Will; I spoke and you believed .... I gave this immense treasure to you and filled your generation with the odour of My fragrance, and every soul that opened the window of her heart to Me was perfumed from within and without, My sweetness penetrating even to the marrow of the bone, fragrancing soul, mind and spirit .... did you not know that when I promise I fulfil?

My child, lean now on the same Heart which My Son, Jesus Christ, is nearest to – and remember: I will cultivate this generation and I will make them understand that immortality is found in being kin to the Triune God; My intention is to draw every soul into a divine and intimate union of love, deifying them in Our one Substance, and in Our one Will ....

O glory be to our Triune God,
God of heaven and earth,
in whose power all creation will bend its knees;
glory be to Him from generation to generation
in the Church;

Let us all proclaim:

there is one Lord, one faith,
one baptism and one God
who is Father of all, through all and within all;

and that there is one true theology:
that of contemplating God in His Triune Glory
and in His Divine Mystery!

be blessed; in the sight of all heaven, I, your Eternal Father, bless you giving you the unction of My Divine Love on your forehead;

30. 11. 1998

*Lord, allow me to find
the promised joy at the end
of the path You have laid out for me;
for this, Righteous Father, teach me
to be dressed by righteousness and courage;
O Lord! Your House is continuously being
battered by rebellion and there is no sign
yet of unifying the dates of Easter;
not really visible; not yet ....
You have turned my life into a sobbing flute
from the moment You've baptised me
by immersing me in the
Lake of Agony of Your Heart!*

*Yes, I know that I have been called by
Divine Power Himself and that
I am in the embrace of a living Defender and that
He will triumph over all the dust of this earth;
but after my awakening, I am still in my flesh –*

O Interpreter of my thoughts,
let not Your harp, as You call me,
be tuned to dirges, for I would commit a sin;
let not Your affection test me
as much as it is testing me now;

daughter, stop babbling; I am right now standing **affectionately** in front of you, reminding you that it is impossible to be in My company without Me sharing with you My Passion and without your traits becoming Mine; ah, and in our intimate union and in our embrace I have given you the unction of My Love to become another living crucifix, another slave to be sold to the world; if I immersed you in what you called rightly the Lake of Agony in My Heart, look what this baptism has brought you, what fragrance, what imperial vestments; I have treated you as I treat My chosen ones;[56]

"behold, I have been clothing you with My Son, Jesus Christ,"

"and I,[57] I who am the Gateway through which the virtuous enter heaven, tell you solemnly: remain as a lily, having been distilled by pure myrrh in that Lake of Agony which in reality represents the Tears of Christ, so that We would say to Our beloved: "how fragrant your perfume, more fragrant than all the other spices, adorned with Our ineffable Light, keep spreading your sweet fragrance so that you find the promised joy at the end of the path We prepared for Our bride, there you will find your lovliest rest in Eternity;"

My Vassula, this agony I have in My Heart is as I have told you[58] before, by force, this generation drags Me into new Gethsemanes;

---

[56] *Suddenly the Father spoke.*
[57] *The Holy Spirit then spoke*
[58] *11.11. 98*

38

what could I have done more that I have not done? although My state was Divine, I emptied Myself to assume the condition of a slave; I served; and to this day they[59] are not satisfied;

My House is in ruin and I, anxious to save My people from ruin, have raised, with My Royal Sceptre, prophets, to assume the condition of a slave and voluntarily serve My House and fortify It, this House I have bought with My Own Blood;

some of My shepherds would ask: "but what are we to do so that our life becomes acceptable to You?" I have been calling you for prayers and for repentance from your hearts so that you reconcile with Me, your God: leave your former style of living and follow Me so that your life becomes acceptable to Me and thus your Knowledge of Our Triune Holiness increases in you; then, allow Us to lead you to contemplate a Spousal contemplation in a Divine intimacy in Our Embrace;

you want to enter into the joy of Our Trinitarian Deity? then call the Holy Spirit, the Giver of Life, the Giver of charisms, the enlightenment of your heart who can fill all things without being contained by their limits, to deploy His Power in your soul ordering all things within you to be renewed; through His benevolent Love and Grace, He will show you His Own Glorious Power by the transfiguration He can perform within you, giving you the strength and grace needed, never to rebel again;

many[60] of you sitting behind your dignitary desks still ask: "why would God intervene when our Church has been enriched so many years now by the Holy Spirit and by so many of our Saints?"

---

[59] *This generation*
[60] *'many' does not mean 'all'*

"to end your rebellion and to end your apostasy", is My reply; in Our gracious condescension We took pity on you; Spring Himself will perfume this earth, fragrancing and reviving with My aroma this apostatized generation ....

and as for unifying the dates of Easter, My Vassula, I am still at their doors waiting, as a beggar waiting for alms, I am still waiting for them to unify those dates ... they keep talking about unity and brotherhood; only conversion of the heart will bring them with humility into the path of unity;

I tell you, I had made known to My apostle Paul by a revelation in his heart, the importance of unity and how to preserve the unity of the Spirit by the peace that binds you all together; I made him understand the order of My gifts as well; I revealed to him that I bestowed on each one of you My favour, allotting it in whatever way; I made it known to him that I went up to the heights, took captives, and gave gifts to humanity; and to some My gift was that they should be apostles, to some prophets; to some, evangelists; to some pastors and teachers, so that all together would with one heart and one voice build up My Body, the Church;

I have raised prophets with My Word and they are **not** those who call themselves theologians who are My prophets, but those whom I lift to My Heart, embedding them well within It to reach the fullest knowledge of Our Divine Will and be able to pronounce Our Will to Our people; I personally pay them tribute with My direct intervention, to prepare them and give them entirely to you all, to admonish you, through My Word I let them know My Will;

My prophets are those who by grace are nourished directly from My Mouth and by placing My Word directly into their mouth;

they come to all of you still dripping with heavenly dew and their words fall on you like refreshing rain;

My prophets' words, that come with My direct intervention are like a sword, to drive the apostatized to repentance, giving Me honour and glory; their words flare like a torch in the darkness of your soul; many of their bones flourish again from the tomb;[61]

if any one asks: "why is our Lord emphasizing the place of His prophets?" tell them this: "our Lord says, 'do not go round My words in order to justify your rationalism; renounce your sin and be happy; may your souls rejoice in the Mercy of your Lord; do not persecute My prophets, for they are My angels consoling with My Word all of you; their function is to warn you and to lead all of you to repentance,' so now is the time of repentance; renounce your sin and find favour with Me;

ah, Vassula, I brought a seed out of Egypt, to plant it where My enemy took away the earth's supply of food; with tenderness and care I cleared a space for it, I anointed it, and planted it; anxious to save My people from ruin I fertilized its soil; it took root and grew into a tree; its branches stretched as far as the sea; its fruit, abundant and succulent; although it was visited often with thunder, hurricanes and fiery tempests, it did not waver;

within three years and a few days My enemy trembled and shuddered; blazing with anger, heavy with threats, he raised an army to sift its fruits with the sieve of destruction to harness them in a bridle; but I gathered each one of them and hid them in My Heart; often as men have attacked My tree they have never overcome it, for My Triune Blessing was on it; ah .... and how

---

[61] *I understood that prophets will never end being sent to us; also the fact that the prophet Elijah never died but was taken up, symbolizes that prophecy will never die.*

often ploughmen have set to work on its back, making furrows to break it, but My right Hand shattered their yoke, throwing them all into confusion;

how blessed the nations that will find shelter under its branches and eat its fruit which I sealed with My Holy Spirit! – the Word of Life was given to you freely so that you, in your turn, My Vassula, give it freely to the dying; woe to those who stretch their hand with fire to destroy what has been planted by Me!

I will continue to cover you with My sweetness, graciously deploying in you like a sweet substance so that the whole world would taste My sweetness; let your accusers pass away like a fading shadow;

I, the Lover of mankind, your Lord and your God, ask to kiss you with the kisses of My Mouth,[62] perfuming you to remain delightful in My Sight;

be good;

ΙΧΘΥΣ ⊂⊃ᕈ

---

[62] *Sg 1 : 2*

1. 1. 1999

The Lord showed me in these past months that I should keep in retreat and enter even more now in holy contemplation. This is also the fruit of union; what more sublime could there be than to be in the embrace of the Holy One? what more pleasing to God could there be than allowing ourselves to be possessed by His Majesty and to learn how to possess Him. The repose of this peace will bring growth in the divine union, strength to continue what the Father laid out for me, zeal and thirst for the salvation of souls;

I noticed too that God was now turning His Gaze more on the services I had rendered Him in spite of my frailty and that His loving instructions were focused on what I should still be doing; the messages in other words were becoming more personal although now and then, God would address His entire Church;

I should have liked also to add that the horror in my soul of being praised by people was becoming so intense that many a times I was at loss with myself and besides myself. Even when I would guess that a person focuses more on me than on the Words of our Divine Master this alone would make me withdraw even more, going even closer in the embrace of God's Love; this special attention given to me sometimes was like a vomit in my eyes .... God made it now clearer to me that any distraction by the world and by people could become a harmful influence that would draw me away from Love's Embrace; the Place I wanted to remain.

I received oceans of graces, oceans of gifts, but have I praised my God enough? have I been negligent on His gifts?

My Vassula, stand firm on what I am transmitting into your intellect and lean on My Heart; I am your Rock; yes,[63] ... I desire you for Myself; during this year I want My beloved to give herself up to the sweet repose of contemplation, withdrawing from the turmoil of the world, entering into My heavenly Embrace; you would be displeasing Me were you to oppose My Will; I want to repose you for My glory but also for the benefit of My Church; come frequently to Me to write down My sayings; I can use you so that My Church renews itself expanding in grace; I had shown you in the beginning My weariness and had asked you if you were willing to repose Me; now I can say:[64]

> "My beloved is My heaven,
> the sweet fragrance of My House,
> who enjoys My favour;
> she is the chant of My angels;
> oh what would I not do for her!"

O infinite and transcendent God,
how could You have from the beginning
gazed on this utterly unworthy and
rebellious creature of Yours?

I, Jesus, am enough to make anyone aware of My Power and My Infinite Mercy .... separate yourself from **this**[65] Fire that emanates from My Heart and you will extinguish; I can keep you ablaze and on fire, vivified by an ardent love for Me, My House and My household; I can bring back to life anyone and lead him with cords of love into perfection ....

---

[63] *This "yes" was a confirmation to my feelings.*
[64] *Our Lord then fondly said these words to me.*
[65] *Jesus emphasized this word, pointing to His Sacred Heart*

44

Lord God, I always feared the praises
of people on me and I always wondered
how these things affected You;
all the while I tried to guard myself against
this worldly fervour because
from the beginningYou made me
understand my utter wretchedness
and how I was the least of them all;

Your Words were like a hammer
hammering in my soul,
engraving them on my heart;
now and then, You reminded me of
my nothingness and that if I dared
lift my chin even for just a moment,
I would lose Your Heart and
all the divine graces too.

In Your exuberant Love
You held me close to Your Heart
and protecting me in this way
You made me understand You,
and that by remaining a nothing
You would take so much pleasure
in this effacement, because You would do
ALL and be ALL!

From my very early childhood
the devil used to appear to me like
a growling black dog ready to tear me into pieces,
but Your all-powerful action protected me;

Your constant Presence guarded me,
leading me in this divine union of Your Heart,
remaining indissolubly united with the Godhead.
Led then by such an indescribable way that
to this day it appears to me as a dream ....

Spouse of souls, I love You!

behold this Heart which chose you, it is the same that was pierced .... you have tasted it, felt it, heard it; still, My own and My child, our work is not finished because My Blood is continuing to stream out of My Heart in rivers;

You are my only Good; what can I do for You?

listen and write: many of My ministers have laid My Vineyard waste and My sheep are scattered; many of them have reduced My House into a ruin, a desolation .... and they know it; there is no peace among them and they know it; I am disappointed with them and this is why they do not want to hear Me; can their vows rid them of their sin?

No, my Lord, I believe not, for sin is sin;

they should observe My ways and repent; then, like a scent of myrrh their perfume will rise up and perfume My House; I, then, will cultivate My sons[66] and will wait with delight for their fine harvest; [67]I confide My Ministers to you .... your Maker will hear your prayers; intercede for them; pray and ask the Father whose forbearance is long to forgive them; do not delay .... do

---

[66] *ministers or shepherds*
[67] *Suddenly our Lord turned to me and when He said: "I confide My ministers to you ..." I felt as though He took off His back the whole Church He was carrying and placed it on my back.*

you not know that even your child-like babblings are heard by the Father and graciously He responds to them? He has granted you so many favours; your advantage being ever so weak, and your very wretchedness makes Him stoop from His Throne;

> *Lord, I offer to You my will and all that*
> *would give more glory to Your Name;*
> *You are my Royal Banquet;*

bringing and giving food to the poor is Our delight; remain in close union to My Heart and listen to its pulsations ....

ic

20. 1. 1999

The Lord gave me a vision: I saw some young boys between 8-10 years of age playing in a very dangerous and foolish way. They were walking on the edge of a ledge which surrounded a tall building of about 7 floors high.

Some of the boys were hiding behind a water pipe-line as though playing hide and seek, all of these games were played from outside the building. Below them were meters of void. Another boy even jumped from his window to just barely make it to the neighbouring building in the window. I shut my eyes, not bearing the thought that I might see one of them miss his step, slip and fall. Considering the height, the fall would be deadly. I was frightened for them and I could not understand why they risked so much their life by playing so dangerously, then I understood why they were fearless; it was because they were not seeing, understanding and realizing the danger.

Vassula, I give you My peace in this week of unity; I, God, have called you to a life of peace; so what have you seen, daughter? what have you observed? have you heard Me say before these words: "do not be afraid of those who kill the body but cannot kill the soul; fear him rather who can destroy both body and soul in hell;" let Me reveal to you this vision: the boys you have seen are some of those who are near you and who had been once prompted by the Spirit to follow My Messages and had offered their help too; today Satan is sifting them and has led them without them realizing to play dangerous games; if they fall, their soul would be fatally wounded; but if they listen to My Spirit they will put an end to their misdeeds and they will live;

well? what was the supreme law I had given you in Scriptures? was it not: "you must love your neighbour as yourself?" to this day all those[68] you have seen in the vision I have given you, think they are righteous, but if they are, let them show it by their good will with humility and graciousness in their actions and by their love for one another; some of them had shown no respect for those who are poor and no respect for the one I chose to bear My Words[69] and carry My Interests; and yes! like in the vision, were you to warn them they would not listen …. and in the meantime like you, in your vision, I too, tremble with fear for their fall could be fatal!

My children, who were called and prompted by the Spirit are now yielding to temptations, yet, were they to allow My Holy Spirit to be their guide, they will be in no danger; for this they need to come to Me and repent; they should not abuse My goodness and My tolerance,

---

[68] *The Lord made them known to me by name.*
[69] *True Life in God*

48

but they should take these instead to lead them to repentance and they will be forgiven and they will not lose My Heart;

I promise that anyone who decides to do good, giving Me honour and will make peace with Me and neighbour, he will obtain peace and will come to realize that in their weakness and in their sleep they were led astray ♡ I want no more trouble from anybody; nor should anyone delude himself into thinking he is righteous, I repeat My warning, do not delude yourselves into thinking **you** are righteous; when one works or had decided to work for Me they should follow Me in My Foot-prints bearing My Cross wholeheartedly and with honour and joy; when this is done with goodwill they will be properly rewarded for all the work that had been done well in My Name;

no one is anyone's master[70] I am the only Master; I urge them to repent and turn to Me and prove to Me their goodwill;

consult Me anytime Vassula, and I shall answer you; I bless you, cling to Hope;[71]

courage daughter; **ic**

This message was given to 2 of the TLIG Associations. I personally did not know that there were disagreements and quarrels; I knew which Associations were concerned after the vision and our Lord made me understand who they were.

---

[70] *In other words Jesus means that there should be no one in a group who works for God become a dictator, ordering others around and 'filtering' everything;*
[71] *It means: "cling to Me."*

There was one especially 'bossing' around everyone; Jesus was not pleased; nor was he with the others. They risked a fatal fall and that is why God intervened out of His boundless Love.

20. 1. 1999

My Vassula: tell Me, is there in the world or around you anything that can give your soul more exquisite and amourous delights than being with Me, just Me, alone? what does My Presence give you?

(While I was searching for words to express myself, I felt the Holy Spirit come upon me ...)

A foretaste of the Beatific vision;
A contemplation of Your Glory;
An indwelling delight, that which is given to the saints with merits; I have none;
An intellectual awareness that in Your transcended light, You, the Godhead, who fill all things without being contained by their limits can dwell in me ....
I find in Your Presence, joy, light, sighs of longing, longing to penetrate even more in contemplation so that I may see what no eye has seen and hear what no ear has heard ...

daughter, hold on to Me and together, My Arm around your arm, just like a bride is led to the altar by her father or a relative to meet her Bridegroom, I will lead you into My Kingdom to reign with Me,[72] surrounded by a throng of exalted angels with an

---

[72] *2 Tm. 2 : 12*

unbounded joy you will be led in eternal glory; and once more all heaven will shout for joy and will sing:

"God has been at work! shout aloud, you earth below! shout for joy you mountains; with royal prodigality the King of kings has found His pleasure in His chosen one; and now let us praise the Lord who created her; exalt the Lord in your praises;"

yes! I have allowed you to hear My Voice; I have allowed you to see Me face to face; and why? why have I favoured you?

To save our generation through Your message?

to show My Infinite Mercy to all of you, and through what I have entrusted you with to carry, I would chime poetry through your mouth at every step you would take and save this generation ....

incense and appeasing fragrance of My Heart, you are not alone, I, your Lord and Saviour am with you; adornment of My Church, lift your eyes up to Me[73] and be blessed ♡

> *My Beloved has put all His Heart*
> *into song out of love for His creation;*
>
> *He placed harps to echo through*
> *the world to*
> *Live a True Life in Him;*
> *brimming over with*
> *Divine Mercy like torrents,*
> *He fills every need;*

---

[73] *When I did, I saw Him whom my heart loves, smiling, showing me once more His dimples ....*

Your Name, O Holy One, most Pure,
reached even the most remote people,
Yes! You have put afire entire nations
with Your divine sweetness,
preventing the people from sinning
and silencing the mutter
of those who oppose You.

have I ever deprived a soul from My Love and Mercy?

Never ....

when I am living inside a city, can that city[74] fall? have you not read: "there is a River[75] whose streams refresh the city of God and it sanctifies the dwelling of the Most High;" I am God;

O Spring of our soul how can I express
the way You have reached us in our misery?
Here you are, offering us
Your Love and Mercy;
like golden pillars on a silver base
You steady our legs;

You transfigure our faces with
one glance of Your Eyes,
making them appear like the Lamp
shining on the sacred Lamp-stand;

Yes, indeed, only the River of Life
whose streams refresh the city of God,
sanctifies it for Him;

---

[74] *God means 'soul'.*
[75] *Holy Spirit*

the Scriptures say,
in fact they are Your Own Words,
Lover of mankind,
that if anyone loves You,
he will keep Your Word
and that Your Father will love him
and that both of You will come to him
and make Your abode with him.
(Jn. 14.23)

I am a Source of ineffable delights and through My Infinite Mercy I wish to transfigure your soul into an Eden, suitable for Our Trinitarian Holiness; I wish to lead every soul back to Myself so that they would have access into their Resting Place; so My Vassula, be determined to safeguard for My sake My teachings; see? the soil has given its harvest, mountains and valleys bow down[76] at My passing; through this revelation My Voice is heard; never mind the proud of heart; remember, My beloved, that I have the power to overthrow kings and kingdoms were these to become an obstacle to Me;

> "peaks of pride, have you the right to look
> down on a mountain[77] where God has chosen to
> live, where Yahweh is going to live for ever?"
> *(Ps 68 : 16)*

My Holy Spirit has uttered sayings in your ear sweeter than honey even than honey that drips from the comb raising you and others from the dead, see? **salvation comes from Me;**

---

[76] *Symbolic: meaning great men of power as well as non-important ones bowed in humility accepting God's intervention;*
[77] *God means, that no one has the right to criticize the one God chooses and in whom He chose to place His dwelling place*

be, My beloved, an example to the others and love My Spirit for He will give you one day the wages of your labours and .... do not fear those who believe they have the power to subjugate all things, because I am with you and on your side;

My Vassula, again I am asking you to be like a lily in My Garden[78] to perfume Me; fragrance Me, My chosen one, I sigh for your love, for your abandonment, for your dispassion;

O you, in whom alone I have entrusted this treasure coming from My Heart![79] remain in My embrace now, perfuming Me in your nothingness and I in My turn will be perfuming you to be My heaven!

hold on fast to Me and on to what I have given you freely; never weary of writing;

I am with you; **ic**

2. 2. 1999

Lord, let me read out to You what St. John Chrysostom wrote. In fact it is Your words, Your words to us through him;

this is what You said:

> *"I, your father, I, your spouse, I, your home, I, your nurse, I, your root, I, your foundation. What ever you want. I will be. You lack*

---

[78] *Our Lord means, His Heart.*
[79] *I heard our Lord say these words aloud and with passion; they came out like a sigh*

*nothing. I will work for you. For I came to
serve and not to be served. I will be your
friend and your host, your head and your
brother, your sister and your mother. I will be
everything. Only be **intimate** with me!*

*I will be poor for you, errant for you, on the
Cross for you, in the tomb for you. Above I
plead with the Father for your sake, on earth I
became intercessor to the Father for your sake.
You are everything for Me, brother, co-heir,
friend and member. What more do you want?"*

I have yielded so many times My Royal Sceptre to reach all of
you and so many times I have come over to you to perfume your
heads; with royal prodigality I have courted you, addressing you
in poetry; religion and virtue were My sweet converse with you
all the days of your life; during all these years[80] I was reposing
My Head on you, I had been taking My delight in you;

My Heart has said of you: "turn her into a living altar for Your
Mystical Body,[81] let her learn to repulse all that does not come
from You, keep her hidden in Us so that she becomes an exultant
sacrifice ready to be sold to the world and serve with gladness;"
I had in My tender affection and My ineffable Love given you
Wisdom to instruct you so that I, through you, would accomplish
My designs on My Church;

see, My beloved, with what intent eagerness I descended upon
your frailty to turn you and through you others to become the
sturdy pillars of My Church? and I, with all My Heart bless you

---

[80] *From the day I opened the door of my heart for our Lord.*
[81] *The Church*

and all those who became columns of divine fire to transmit My words in these urgent Messages and who voluntarily with love used all that they could, with unsparing love and fervour to propagate the Truth and christianize this dechristianized population; I am with you; and I promise you that I will repay you and the others a hundredfold;

see how I raise ambassadors of peace and see how I rush over to rescue My House? see My Vassula, My Eyes are too pure to rest on rebellion; the splendour of My Work, (for My Work it is,) is to draw all souls in My Sacred Heart; if I were not to hurry, raising with My Sceptre disciples, the fig tree will not blossom; nor will there be any fruit left on the vine, and My sheep will continue to scatter until there will be none left in the fold; Goodness and Mercy could not bear to see so many souls heading for the eternal fires;

ceaselessly and untiringly, with My Heart in My Hand, I will continue to look at the window of each heart to awaken it and bring it into the ardent Love of My Divinity;

then I will place all the virtues needed with a stream of unparalleled and sanctified graces on its altar to draw it into a complete union with the Father, Me and the Holy Spirit, immersing it into the eternal joys of heaven, and into Our delights;

now I am telling you, everything where you are[82] passes away like a shadow, but My Words will never pass away;[83]

---

[82] *That means on earth.*

[83] *Here our Lord started to say the following words as one who utters an oath, in solemnity but at the same time as a command.*

"I shall augment your zeal for My House and the fire I shall put within you shall disarm the great; let this Source within you never run dry; may you continue eagerly and with avidity to defend the Truth and My Church which I bought with My Own Blood; let the scourge of your persecutors never discourage you or wear you out, but let this vile act done to you make you stronger instead, by inhaling from My Mouth the graces you need to keep your soul tranquil and in peace;"

ah, generation, greater profit than this Book[84] for your so miserable times you could not have received; greater gift for My Church for its renewal She could not have received, but once more My Church is failing Me, for She has not understood My intentions ....

come, Vassula, the Anointed One will provide you shelter in His Sacred Heart; **love Me equally as I love you**; come, My Own, and perfume My Heart; I promise you that one day I will take you to see the sweet fruits of your labours and you will rejoice ....

now come to Me and recite your prayers, I am always moved by your prayers; come and inebriate Me with your prayers;

> *I am now speechless Lord;*
> *for what do You always find in this*
> *worthless and useless heart of mine*
> *to pour in it divine words*
> *sweeter than honey-comb?*

I esteem an innocent soul no matter how wretched she could be, more than sceptres and thrones; have you not said the other day

---

[84] *Jesus means: "True Life in God" volumes*

that you felt like a mother towards Me? a mother who would do anything to protect her child from being constantly hurt, ridiculed and abused by the world? your love for Me touched Me, it has exceeded your misery ....

My Celestial Liturgy,
it is You, the Godhead
who encompasses all beings,
who clothed me with royal vestments
to be able to walk in and out of Your Courts;

You anointed me
so as to converse with You face to face
stirring my heart with Your noble theme;

You fed me with Goodness and Sweetness
and offered me a royal banquet
so that everything be distributed for all the nations
with largesse and with royal prodigality;

Was it not You that in Your divine munificence
poured into me the flow of Divine Love,
resurrecting me?

God of all Goodness, Sweet Spirit of Grace,
Most Loving Lover of Mankind,
who knew and knows all my
defects, deficiencies and vileness, how in spite of all these
"morbid worms"
You still are gracious to me and approach me;

Luminous Manifestation, I give praise and honour to You
and ask You to pity always my wretchedness and my
unworthiness;   Kyrie eleisson;

ah, Vassula, whenever you are mindful of your frailty and of your wretchedness knowing that Life can only be drawn from Me, I rejoice; whenever you admit that you are a sinner and that only by your total abandonment to Me you could draw graces from Me, I can then proceed in you and My Will can be accomplished in you;

transfigured by the grace of the Breath of My Holy Spirit, I will indeed proceed My intentions in you;

I, Jesus, bless you, be one;   **ic**

5. 2. 1999

What return can I make to
the Almighty's Goodness
He showed to me?
He has performed marvels in me;

I have built My Throne in you to outlast all time …. I am Your King who anointed you so that you enter into My Kingdom; I am the King of the safety of your soul;

My heart melts like wax and
becomes liquid in Your Divine Presence;
I rejoice in Your Splendour and Majesty;
You have demonstrated Your Power
by allowing Your Holy Presence
to flow through the desert of my soul like a river;
alleluia! and everything that was polluted
in the aridity of my soul was washed away
in the greatness of Your Love;

yes, My beloved, I am known for My Mercy and for My tender Heart; have you not heard how I can turn deserts into rivers and arid grounds into springs of water? extol Me at the meetings and make this generation understand that Royal Dignity is Mine;

what return can they make to Me for My Sovereignty?

My Royal Heart raises the poor in spirit, I lift the needy and the wretched to give them royal vestments allowing them to walk in My Courts; I bless them by imprinting My Holy Name all over them opening the gates of virtue to them so that their behaviour pleases My Royal Dignity; schooled by Me they will learn how to lead a blameless life;

> *I shall proclaim in all assemblies*
> *the greatness of Your Name,*
> *without fear I shall cry out that*
> *Mercy is with us,*
> *stooping from the heavens to reach us;*

> *and to those who hound me, lovingly intervene;*
> *rescue me from human oppression;*
> *support me as You have promised me*
> *and let the foul and lying tongue be subdued;*

have you noticed any limitations? go on, say it ….

> *am I wrong if I say: on the "inner walls"*
> *of Your House, there, I find not much of a support …*

no one will be able to strike you down not even the "inner walls", as you have called them, of My House, so long as I am with you and by your side;

the "inner walls" would have closed over you, but the masons who toiled to build those "inner walls" have toiled in vain; your mere zeal for My House which devours you will topple them ...

I have not asked you whether you had support on the "inner walls" of My House or not; I have asked you if you have noticed any limitations ...

> *No; not in the whole;*
> *Your Message is expanding,*
> *and I see Your Glory and Your Power;*
> *great are Your achievements, my God;*
> *You have let Your children see Your Glory;*
> *You rule over everything ...*
> *and You are expanding*
> *Your Holy Message of True Life in God ....*

so do not fear; whosoever bows you down, I will raise you up again; I have raised you up to be My pupil; it is I, your Bridegroom, so come, enter into the joy of your Lord!

listen carefully and write:

to this day My Merciful Calls have not been given much attention,[85] neither have My warnings been regarded; My pupil, My Return is imminent, I have sent you out to proclaim My Words in this world, and to speak in My Holy Name but many still would not listen;

Satan's hour is coming to an end for My triumph is near; this is why he holds so many captive, bound with apostasy; bound with falsehood;

---

[85] *Not as much as it was expected*

generation! generation your apostasies have been many but greater than this one I have not seen and today this evil generation refuses to listen to My Merciful calls and continues to follow the dictates of their own hardened hearts, shrugging their shoulders they say, My daughter: "we prefer to do as we please ..." and they settle for evil .... since they have abandoned the Fountain of Living Water they shall die in their apostasy;

My Father is more than offended; how much longer will the earth be divided and riven? how much longer will My Church be divided and in rebellion?[86] the Spirit of My Father is constantly blasphemed and ridiculed by many of My ministers; has this generation not yet heard an uproar from heaven? have you not yet heard from the highest heaven a lamentation from the saints?

ah, Vassula to see these souls[87] delight in their abomination, how would heaven not claim vengeance? and I would add with tears in My Eyes, that many of My Church's dignitaries trust more on what is thought highly of by men, yet forget that by Me these things are loathsome in My Sight;

I ask you solemnly: do I not fill heaven and earth? will I not then pour out My Holy Spirit on all mankind and carry out My Promise?

and so I tell all those who follow the dictates of their hardened hearts: "since you do not see the earth being filled with the brightness of the glory of My Spirit, and you continue to call evil what is good and holy, by your own incredulity you will draw upon your heads your own sins;"

blessings on him who believes, may they enter into My Joy!

---

[86] *I heard at the same time: unreconciled and not in peace.*
[87] *the souls: the generation which apostatized.*

I would not like anyone to fall in the path of delusion and believe that My Father's wrath has diminished; His Mercy is great but His severity is as great; and ah, generation, how can you escape damnation? what you have been sowing all these years you will reap ....

so, Vassula, your race is not over, extol My Name in My assemblies;[88] I have given you a spiritual gift to be able to turn the hearts of fathers towards their children and the hearts of children towards their fathers; many would profit from your gift, and from your labours;

those who will listen will receive in their hearts sanctifying graces and by these graces much of the rust of their sins would be healed, because they would have been those who had welcomed My Holy Spirit of Grace;

these times are the times in which Scriptures[89] speak of My Day and of a devouring fire, when the sky will break into flames, and woe for the unrepented heart! how much more could I have warned you, generation?

My divine visitation is imminent and the Fire of the Purification is nearing in which your souls would melt like wax, by its heat; I have offered you, generation, and I am still offering you the condescension of My intimate and divine friendship, but you have not accepted it and many of you have not understood what the Bridegroom was offering you;

daughter, remember that I have you enveloped into My special care; have you not heard the testimonies of those[90] I had given

---

[88] *The Lord means, in the prayer meetings.*
[89] *2 Peter : 3 : 1 - 18*

the grace to see My Countenance on you, invigorating them with My appearance? so do not underestimate My divine Power;

I will continue to show Myself on you, adorning you with My Countenance for this pleases My Father;

keep your eyes fixed on your frailty, your wretchedness, your imperfections and your so many misgivings, then graciously give Me always the liberty to demand from you your time and your willingness to christianize this dechristianized society of yours, interceding lovingly as well for the Unity of My Church;

let your sole interest be on My Interests; plead for the conversion of sinners; these prayers offered to Me are like an aromatic fragrance of incense; this [91]sigh of yours fragranced My Heart and it was My pleasure to receive it ...

love Me and make reparations for those who recrucify Me daily .... enjoy My Presence, I am with you;

I, Jesus bless you;

ic

---

[90] *Many people in different nations witnessed Christ's Holy Face appear on my face.*
[91] *Suddenly I gave a sigh for I knew my mission given to me by the Most High; To plead, to make reparations, and trot the world evangelizing, without rest, so that my life turns into an unceasing prayer and sacrifice.*

Lent 3. 3. 1999

Lord?

I Am .... naha lishbu firü nabish khaleh shbekh nirü malekh bissä; mbarakh abshan khedir lah coghar;[92]

I am your Saviour, your All, your Heaven; blessed is he who receives Me; have my Peace ♡ I, Jesus bless you;

it is marvelous to see you depend entirely on My Power! I would hate to see you become habitual and not depend on grace; see? My Divine Presence how distinct it is when I am in communication with you?

Vassula, hear and write: "your salvation lies in conversion and tranquility;" this was one of My Themes that I was addressing to all of you in these past years; but in return for what the Bridegroom[93] was offering, He still receives hostility and disdain;

He calls out and says: "My Return is imminent, be prepared to receive Me in grace while Grace is still at your very doors!" but in your lethargy, generation, your darkness continues to increase in you, growing ever more arrogant; My Light is shining so bright, yet in your obscurity, generation, no one sees it; here I come to illuminate your dreadful night but to this day My Holy Spirit is not honoured;

you fill yourselves, generation, with all that is not holy and is an abomination in My Eyes, you hear of emissaries sent from Me,

---

[92] *All of this was given to me with an unknown language*
[93] *Jesus calls Himself 'The Bridegroom' in this passage.*

and you show your gratitude by raising your hands calling out your praises to Me for sending them as 'ambassadors of the Most High' to be among you; but instead of pondering over My Words, your endurance is affected by your inclinations towards sensationalism; these people are like Scriptures say of them: "they are like a drowsy man, besotted with sleep whom you are trying to rouse up, having explained to him certain things, when you have finished he will say, 'what is it all about?' his heart, like a broken jar will not hold any of My given knowledge, then, like a fool he is led astray;"

this is why Satan has raised so many false prophets, who ape[94] My teachings and My divine actions; so many of you are reading what does not come from Me but are of human origin and a false creation by the evil one; but I will call all hidden deeds, good or bad, to judgement; I called out from the very beginning: "come all of you who wander in this desert and discover Me, your Triune God;"

see, there is no closed door from My side, but My Calls are not heeded nor are they honoured; My frequent visits to you, together with My chosen one, bringing all the way to your feet My Salvific Love Hymn to renew you and restore My tottering House, have been left uncultivated;

to some of you, I said: "I will now strip you of My visits since you seem to be indifferent to My request of multiplying the fruits of her labours in your hands by evangelizing;" and so I have; moreover, this departure and abstinence is necessary for your growth; this is the hour, or never, to take up the sickle and reap vigorously; reap a harvest you never prepared yourself and have My blessings;

---

[94] *I understood that some are copying even these messages.*

Vassula, My adoptive child, learn that We[95] are constantly by your side, transforming you through loving union; I have immersed you in My limpid springs,[96] that flow from My Mouth to teach you Wisdom, penetrating you in Us for a deeper understanding of Our Triune Deity; therefore, who could have given you such tranquility, such freedom of the spirit, who could have covered you with sapphires?[97] and now who is giving you rest in His Arms withdrawing you from creatures?

from the beginning I have sent you, with royal prodigality, still dripping from My limpid springs, to be among the wretched and the poor; you have germinated in My springs, and as Moses, whom I had enveloped by a cloud I have you enveloped in My Arms in a holy contemplation, during which your soul and mind are lifted in the Divine;[98]

in My benevolence and the ineffable condescension of My Love I have given you now and then glimpses of the Beatific Vision; to keep you happy I have appeared on you, sometimes like a transparent veil, and at other times I englobed you entirely, to show that you come from My limpid springs;

to encourage you I have given signs in your assemblies and wonders to accompany you and the mission I have given you; this generation has been witnessing dazzling wonders;

ah![99] if only some would value more the treasures We have been pouring on them … I[100] am the vivifying substance of your soul

---

[95] *The Holy Trinity*
[96] *The Word of God*
[97] *Sapphires, represent here, virtues.*
[98] *In God*
[99] *This was a sigh from God*
[100] *Suddenly the Holy Spirit uttered these words*

and He who brought you into a filial love with Our Divinity to lead a divine life and become another child, by adoption, of the Father; I am the Sovereign Master of your soul but your Friend as well, giving you access to free speech, allowing you to express your opinion, your thoughts and your free will which I have restored to you;

so you see My Vassula, what it is like to be a daughter by grace as the Word is Son by nature?

you have been called to participate in this Divine Salvific Plan but to enter as well in the Triune life; come and breathe in Me and fill your soul with Our Divine Love, this Divine Love that draws you into a perfect union with Us ♡[101]

listen, My chosen one, I know how diligent you are when it comes to My Interests and My Glory; I know too how much sacrifice you offer to the world to convert and how devout and eager you are to console Me when you see Me stretching out My Hand imploring, beseeching My House to unite by reconciling and making peace, and I know too how you feel when you see Me tearful for the rejection I get;

but now, in My turn, I want once more to reassure you of the favours I granted you and of My affection I have for you; yes, I know too how My absences[102] can leave you in pain even though they are not of long duration but are temporary,

Ah my Anointed One,
my mind still cannot conceive Your absences
without being anguished

---

[101] *Jesus continued*
[102] *In the sense of not receiving a call*

ah, but I have sworn an oath which I never will retract, this of ending your mission together, of never abandoning you;

victory is near, for the Power of My Love is far greater than the power of evil and all hell put together; so rejoice and allow Me to keep you in My service, keep your ears opened to the Voice of Holy Wisdom; it is My ardent wish to instruct you and then I can complete on you the Divine Work I had started;

cloistered in Me, in My Heart, I want you to be in a permanent state of contemplation in which your soul remains tranquil and inebriated with My sweetness; keep aspiring from My Heart My revelations and instructions, so that you forward them to this generation and for all others to come; ♡ the Holy Spirit will continue to favour you with His Sublime Light into your intellect and through this Light you will embellish My Church; remain small, truly small, allowing His power of action to be even more efficacious; profess the Creed with love and proceed in Our Light and never doubt of Our Wealth, of Our Mercy and of Our Tenderness shown to you;

My Father has opened your heart by a mere glance of His, like a sharp ray of light that incises, He opened your heart and filled it with Our luminous and Divine Light, revealing Our Image within you, turning your heart into Spring, renewing you with a flow of virtues, renewing Our sanctuary and Our domain so that you may be the just herald who would allow Us to engrave on you Our Love Hymn, enriched with boundless mystical knowledge and understanding;

come, My Divine Plan will be accomplished in you with Tenderness and not with sorrow; receive My blessings and do not fear; I have engaged you for this apostolate of Unity and by engaging you I honoured you to engage you to My Cross so that you may absorb all its phases; embrace It with love and remember Its victory!

I, Jesus, who am near you, bless you ♡ **ic**

> *The Spirit of God speaks through me,*
> *His word is on my tongue, He embedded me*
> *in His Heart like a precious stone on a crown,*
> *He stooped from His Throne to lay on my path*
> *a bed of roses; You have yielded Your Sceptre*
> *to a non-existent creature never caring whether this*
> *merciful gesture of Yours would cheapen Your Sceptre;*

> *I have been taught learnings of the*
> *Sages in Your Bosom,*
> *from a filthy rag*
> *You've turned me into Your herald,*

> *Blessed is Your Name, Amen*

9. 3. 1999

> *The Spirit of God revealed to me how*
> *one becomes a child of God;*
> *being thus freed, we can now enjoy*
> *the same freedom and glory as*
> *the rest of the other children of God.*
> *The Spirit of Love has unfolded in front*
> *of my eyes the Glory of the Triune God*
> *with all Their Splendour and Treasures.*
> *And now I can say with tranquility in my soul:*

"The Spirit has captured my soul
and turned me into His belonging, and
at the same time gave me my real freedom.
In His Grace He offered me a Royal Festival,
He offered Himself to me;

Then, like a River, He flowed in me,
renewing me without ceasing, renewing my
union with the Triune God;

Supplier of all gifts,
You have given me Your friendly Flame
communicating with me in Person,
bringing me to the Father and to the Son,
uniting my soul to them as well;

Divine Flame of my heart,
You who transfigured Your abode
to Your taste to satisfy Yourself and
satisfy me, I now shout for joy!

I can hear now a Voice
and I can no longer say: 'I do not recognize';
I feel a Breath sliding over my face
and I cannot deny that Someone is standing
before me, smiling, shining,
how can I say:
'I am not in the presence of the Divine?'

Now I have opened my mouth
but my tongue shaped those words
through the Spirit and if my heart will utter
words of wisdom, again it will be
through the Spirit of Grace;

My Vassula,[103] I want equality of love ....

love Me and aspire from Me all the divine inspirations which belong to the sons and daughters of the Most High; I have set Our dwelling-place[104] in order, I have put everything straight, because I am a God of order; I have been visiting you as I did with the Apostles to restore Our sanctuary[105] for Our good pleasure, then I have set My Throne inside you; I revealed My gifts and My treasures to you, and I adorned you with My mere Presence, it pleased Me to possess you, and pour in you My Wisdom so that your soul shines forth in splendour; I have immersed you in Our limpid springs, to revive you;

Notebook 98

- and I can say now:

> *"I found rest, and I am enjoying Your Riches;"*
> *even when I depart from this earth*
> *I will leave these Treasures for future generations*
> *that are to come;*

it is a trifle for Me to cover you with My Wealth; have you not heard that God never ceases to give Himself to all of you?

even as I am ceaselessly giving Myself to everyone, so will it be with you when I would prepare you to meet your Bridegroom; you would be giving yourself to the Lover of mankind, becoming one spirit with the Divine; like a true son and daughter of God, you would become in this elevated state of grace a perfect image of the Triune God, and all your undertakings will be done without

---

[103] *Holy Spirit speaks*
[104] *my soul*
[105] *my soul*

any flaw, since they would be divine and according to Our Mind and Our Will;

even, My Vassula, your movements will be changed into Ours; every gesture, every step you will take in your life will be done in Our Love and they will keep amplifying by grace; as a daughter, a true daughter of the Most High, your spirit will be immersed in Our Divinity;

it is I, sweet daughter, who brought you into this filial love and into this Divine union, expanding your heart to receive more of Us so that We receive more of you, to give Ourselves more to you so that you give yourself more to Us; in this cycle you will be giving Us all that belongs to Us already; this is My triumph in you, the triumph of having brought you, after you had given Me your free will, into a perfect union of Divine Love with Us;

see how good it is to surrender? how could I have fulfilled My actions otherwise?

Sovereign Master I am now in your soul, but as I have told you once before, I am not only a Sovereign Master, but your Friend and Beloved as well; I have built you up to become a child of God who, being Our offspring, as any offspring, would have the right as well to share and give its opinion; even to govern with His Father;

in the tranquility of My Breath in you, you will see things through Our Light and the way We see them; so I am telling everyone:

be rich in poverty, and I
will turn a favourable Eye on you,

let me call you as well,
son or daughter of the Most High,
and you will rule with Us;

allow Me to set you on your feet
to enable you to move in Me;

allow Me to set My Throne in you so that you too can say to others: "I have found rest ..." have you no desire to see your Father? do you not languish to meet God?

if you do, then I must give you birth, yes, you have to be reborn of Me to see your Father; no child has ever seen his father before being born;

happy the man who meditates on the Freedom I can give; this Freedom will carry you as a Bridegroom carries His Bride into perfecting your union with Us; the transfiguration of love imprinted on your soul will be such that henceforth nothing will be able to separate you from Us ♡

*Our Lord is filling us
with Knowledge and Understanding
revealing to us good and evil;*

*What more can one ask for?
The Most High has established
His School in our hearts,*

As a Light it shines from
within and without;
He stoops from His Throne
to show us the magnificence
of His works;

And as He set Knowledge before us,
He sets His Throne within us;
adorning our soul majestically
with His Presence;
Holy is His Name;

What is man to assess God?
and yet many of them do;

How can it be possible for any man
to fathom His Greatness and His Marvels?
and yet some think they can;

Being too ready to show they know
shows their shallowness of mind;

This is why the Holy Spirit
conceals His Treasures from them,
and keeps them for the lowly;

Yes, Lord, in every way
You have made it known, through ages,
that You exalt the lowly
and the proud of heart You rout;
You have never disdained the poor in spirit,
but stood by them always and everywhere.

25. 4. 1999

It is known that You, my God,
take always the side of the virtuous:

So please, give my eyes light,
let my heart rejoice in You, Lover of mankind;

Lord, You, in all Your Sovereignty bent the heavens
all the way to my room and You came down;

You left Your Throne

God is inside His city now and she will not fall as long as He
lives in her ....[106]

My heart and soul have been
nourished by the King;
(I answered the angels)

yes![107] the King has favoured you, moved by your wretchedness,
He yielded His Royal Sceptre to address His poem to you and
bless you; come! meditate on God's marvels ....

Ah ... my heart has become
like liquid in His Presence;
how can I forget God's Tenderness?
how can I forget His marvellous kindness?

---

[106] *Suddenly angels appeared and with great joy, almost like a melody*
said these words.
[107] *Again the angels responded*

I[108] am on your side; My glance is on My chosen one; I have blessed you for you are one of those who sprouted from My Heart, still dripping with myrrh; I have engraved all over you these words: "Your Lord God desires equality of Love from you;"

yes, I alone can clothe you in My splendour and give you the indispensible Light; I alone, in My Divinity can impress upon your soul My Image of Holiness; it is I, your God who can perfect you and lift you to travel with Me in My company; come to Me and prolong your gaze on My Holy Face so that you may understand fully that you are joint heiress with Me, united to Me and in Me .... receive, daughter – of – the King,[109] more of Me, allowing Me to receive more of you;

My wish is to give more of Myself to you, so that you can give more of yourself to Me; I will be obtaining in this way all that belongs to Me already; through My Divine Love that will be poured in you, you will be deified, transfiguring your soul, so that My Father identifies you on Judgement Day with Me;

in your so miserable times, generation, where sin has become your master and is being poured in you like venom, I, the Master of Love and Mercy, pour in abundance on you, to heal you, the antidote, that is My Holy Spirit; I pour in abundance on you My Mercy, with anointed Messages from the Treasures of My Heart; I am the Divine Source of Graces;

he who journeys in the dark will end up his journey in the dark; he who chooses to journey in the light will end up his journey in the light; **I am the Light** of the world; anyone who follows the

---

[108] *The Lord God spoke now.*
[109] *Which in Greek is: Vassiliki*

Light will not be walking in the dark, but will radiate the light of life; **I am the Life** ….

generation, why, why do you torment your soul in those obscure regions of Satan, subduing your will to his evil designs? **I am the Way, the Truth and the Life** and it is through Me you could enter heaven;

if you say you are weak, come to Me and draw strength from Me so that one day you too will be able to chant: "my Triune God, has shone in my heart; the Living God has given me, the unworthy one, a spiritual resurrection, and as Moses was enveloped by a cloud, I am being enveloped by mystical learnings coming from Holy Wisdom; and as the sun inundates the creation with its light, my Lord and my God has inundated my soul with His Teachings and has poured in me torrents of Divine Love; He has given me instructions and knowledge again through Holy Wisdom, to understand His Glory and to comprehend that He is The Divine Bridegroom of all His creation; His exuberant Love drew my soul into the nuptial chamber of His Heart where a divine union was performed; then my Beloved rose, afire with majestic Love to show me His Treasures; and in this nuptial chamber, where my Beloved keeps all His Treasures, I discovered:

- the treasure of knowing and understanding God;
- the treasure of intimacy;
- the treasure of joy and consolation;
- the treasure of the path of virtues;
- the treasure of the Holy Spirit;
- the treasure of Holy Wisdom, an inexhaustible treasure to men;
- the treasure of sweet converse with the Divine;

yes, indeed, the Lover of mankind has enriched me with His Love and filled my heart with His inexhaustible treasures;"

Love compels Me to yield My Royal Sceptre, taking pity on this generation's desolation;   Love compels Me to deploy limitless Mercy on your aridity, generation, leading Me to bend all the way to you and cover you with My precious Blood to conceal your imperfection;

now, My Vassula, I will have you converse with My Mother ....

call in mind My child the pierced side, feet and hands of your Saviour, Jesus Christ, who eternally sits on the right hand of God the Father and reigns in Glory;   Jesus and I are in constant intercession for the salvation of souls;   My Immaculate Heart too is pleading the Father to obtain His Mercy for this generation; here I am grieving again for the injustice done to so many of My children,[110] increasing God's Cup of Justice;   I need acts of reparation and prayers to remedy this evil;   cry out to the Father and say:

"Father, forgive them for they know not what they are doing;"

then come and cloister yourself in My Royal Heart;   there you will find your peace but at the same time you will taste and feel My agony and sorrow in the depths of My being as I am moved by what I see;   I see this flow of ceaseless evil, without a moment's interruption, which comes from Satan;

to put an end to all of this, I need from all of you acts of reparation and constant prayers .... without repentance evil will increase;

---

[110] *(Our Blessed Mother was referring the Kosovo crisis)*

God is sending Me in these days to all of you to transmit His Grace for a renewal of your heart; My maternal Love is grace to you as well;

be good ♡

> *Grant O Heavenly Mother*
> *the Grace of God on us all, so unworthy,*
> *to be able to ask God sincerely pardon*
> *for our sins and the sins of others;*
>
> *Grant us the inestimable treasure*
> *of God's intimate friendship, and the*
> *noblest treasure of the divinity which is*
> *the closeness to God : God offering*
> *His Heart to all of us;*
> *Amen;*

I bless you; and forgive[111] all those who cast stones at you; I want you fair,[112] and seek God's ways always;

21. 6. 1999

[113]My daughter, in order to elucidate certain sayings of Mine and to progress your soul into the depths of Wisdom and of the knowledge of Myself, I appear to be repeating Myself sometimes, but this is one way of edifying your soul, progressing it gently into sanctity;

---

[111] *I was asked to forgive my oppressors.*
[112] *I understood, beautiful (spiritual beauty)*
[113] *The Father speaks*

I am pouring in you, since you have given Me, your God, the required space (in you,) quantities of My Graces for the benefit of the Church; nothing of what I have written will go in vain; in fact the Church will fulfill its needs; I have raised you with royal prodigality, no, I have not raised you because I have found you worthy but I have called you by the free gift of My Grace and it is in My Justice that I grant these Graces; no one is innocent enough and worthy to receive from Me such royal prodigalities;

never tire studying the pages of all the notebooks I filled, for they are brimming with knowledge and with the sweetness of My Heart, unveiling My Beauty by enhancing it in your soul ... I shone inside you, I shone a brilliant light within you to wake you up so that you leave behind[114] you all the world's trivialities; I performed prodigies in you to sing poetry to Me; to extend My Kingdom in you I poured Myself in you, lifting your soul into a spiritual jubilation, so that I hear from My chosen one My Own Canticle of Love; and thus, all that you received of Divine value returns to Me, the Author of Prodigies;

ah, Vassula, when I raise souls by Grace in that mysterious way and they see what eye has never seen and hear what ear has never heard and learn things beyond the mind of man, I am glorified in My Glory; and as I advance in your nothingness taking delight at every step I take, I approach My aim of bringing your soul to My demand, and that is: **equality of My Love;**

no one can ever reach on earth that height of My Love; you will say: "then why does My God who transcends greatness and

---

[114] *I understood also, 'empty yourself from'*

fullness, demand something of me that I cannot fulfill?" **I only demand what belongs to Me already,**[115]

I have sent you My Holy Spirit to dwell in you and make Our Love known to you, transfiguring your soul to desire Us, to be able to declare with delight: "I possess God, and He possesses me!" My Vassula, one has to receive this inestimable grace, to pronounce these words, words spoken so sweetly, motivated by the Spirit of Love, whom you allowed to dwell in you;

have you not heard, that the Word of God is something alive and active: it cuts like any double-edged sword but more finely: it can slip through the place where the soul is divided from the spirit;[116] so, daughter, love Me as much as I love you and as perfectly as you can with the love that My Holy Spirit has so graciously infused in you, you will only be giving Me back what belongs to Me already;

in the beginning[117] I had asked you to love Me, and you answered: 'I love you ...' and in My smiles I said: 'love Me more ...' now My Holy Spirit progressed you to get to know Me and love Me bringing you to Me, as a bride is brought to her bridegroom and perform an everlasting union; in that same manner, but in a more ineffable way, the Holy Spirit brought you to an everlasting union of love with Us and in Us the Triune God;

---

[115] *In other words, after having given our will to God, He fills us with the Holy Spirit of Love to love. This love, no matter to what degree it is, belongs to God, for He gave it.*
[116] *Heb. 4 : 12*
[117] *The first communications, back in 1985*

You are the Great Godhead,
the Almighty, the awe-inspiring God,
You are the incomprehensible Splendour,
surpassing all the splendours of Your Angels
put together; You, who fill all things
without being contained neither by
their limits nor by their very being;

My hand trembles in front
of Your Divine Majesty while I am writing;
how to this day, Lord, could I conceive
in my little mind still that the
Prodigious Prodigy of prodigies
Himself is in familiar communication
with me daily and converses with me
in this delightful manner?
How do you want me to fully understand
in my wretchedness, O Lord, that You,
the Unseen God,
the One who encompasses all beings,
is speaking to me with such
sweetness and tenderness?
what mind is able to grasp this prodigy?

You have blessed me with the
unction of Your Name to save me
and others through
Your Hymn of Love;

You have blessed me by a
triple Resurrection Kiss and
made me a close partner of
Your Salvific Plan;
Can anyone come to me and say:

"I can measure the magnificence
of God and His inexpressible grandeur";
No one can say this, because
my Lord and my God is a
fathomless Well of hidden and
unknown Treasures;

indeed I Am .... We[118] have been calling you to rest in Our Arms, like a child in his mother's arms, you are called as a child by grace, to share in Our Salvific Plan, you are all called to become gods by participation and enter in the Triune life to rule with Us; indeed I am Sovereign of your soul, oh, but such an intimate Friend as well, who can draw you into deification;

in spite of your awesome wretchedness, at this moment while I am with you in this way, and you, while you are with Me in this way, enveloped in a holy contemplation, not even the most solemn festivals given in My honour are as delightful and pleasing to Me as in these moments of your contemplation; when My Divine Presence is with you, I rejoice in the presence of the one whom I have made to become the bone of My Bone, the flesh of My Flesh; I, by My Own Hand raised a sanctuary, would I then not enjoy My Own good Work?

Kindest Lover of mankind,
You are once more sounding
like music to my ears;

God of unfailing Fidelity,
You who are moved by
creatures like me who have
a crust of rust all over,

---

[118] *The Holy Trinity*

You do not hesitate to cry out loudly
in the heaven before
anyone makes a move:

"she is acquitted!"

how is it possible then not to melt
in love in Your Presence?
and go out, running
with both hands raised up
shouting at every cross-road:

"My Creator is my Liturgy!"

You have displayed
Your Mercy from the earliest times;
You are my Maker
superbly Beautiful and Gracious;

Your Mercy, my Lord,
is ever so great that
the most intelligent elite
in the Church will still sound
like a fool if he tries to explain it;

come, beloved, enter into the joy of your Lord;

you have heard the Messages of your salvation (given to you) bestowing upon you at the same time a variety of gifts of My Grace; in the Power of the Holy Spirit exercise all that I have given you and do not get discouraged for I am with you;

I am reminding you, little grain, that you are fighting in the same battle as all My Prophets fought; gales can blow on you, floods can rise to drown you, but nothing of these will overcome you, for I am with you and in My good care to withstand your frailty;

lean on Me; and do not despair on the situation of the Church; ecclessia will revive!

I am before you ♡

30. 6. 1999

I have been teaching you these days with delight, how all My sons and daughters can become gods by participation if they allowed Me to flow in them My Divine Love; I want to extend My Reign in them and take possession of them, as I want them to take possession of Me;

if they would not contradict My Holy Spirit, He will take possession of them, and turn them into a blossoming garden; He will fill them with virtues and perform marvels within them to build up in them the fullness of Christ; if they allow Me to flow Myself in them I will turn them into adoptive sons and daughters of Mine;

My Grace I reveal to you and salvation has been given to you through My Son, Jesus Christ; in order to set you free, He sacrificed Himself for you; in order for you to share a Divine

Life, He constituted the Holy Eucharist to sanctify you and partake of His Body and Blood; you are not partaking any mere bread or wine, but you are partaking God Himself; if you would only reflect on this Mystery and understand it fully!

the Inaccessible God is Accessible to you, the Invisible God is visible to you, and ready to divinize you; He whose grandeur surpassess all angelic forces and all beings and all that has been created, is at your disposal, creation! God Himself is being offered to you to give you back your divinity, divinizing your soul to enter Eternal Life;

if you allow Me to flow in you, I will make you understand all those things which are invisible to you, in order to bring your soul into a full repentance; this repentance will transform your so miserable sullied state into a pure, dignified transformation of body and soul, ready then to partake the One you think Unattainable and Inaccessible;

He who glories at My right Hand, He whom you call, daughter, 'my Liturgy!' gives Himself to you, to eat His Flesh and drink His Blood in order that you become the flesh of His Flesh, the bone of His Bone;

I will execute at any time and to anyone who wishes, My act of Love, if they cry out to Me:

"come, and make me Your property
and your adoptive child!"

and before anyone makes a move in Heaven, My cry will be heard by everyone:

"acquitted!"

then you too, My child, will sprout from My springs and become god by participation;

I will not be like a ship that cuts through heaving waves and leaves no trace to show where it passed, no, I will let everyone hear you and know that the Triune God now lives in you and is hidden in you; Our vivifying passage within you will not go by un-noticed for you will praise Me saying:

"I have learned how to possess God, from My Father; God is my Father, it is He who fathered me and made Himself known to me without losing His transcendence; He, whose Magnificence is magnified in all His creation has filled me with His Knowledge; the Triune God who encompasses all beings, filling all things with His brightness without being contained by their limits, offered Himself to me, ordering all things within me to be good; and now my soul is content and satisfied for being filled, in spite of my wretchedness, with God;"

yes, be happy! be happy all you who hear the melody of My Voice and have your fill in Me;

> *ah, my Lord, Your baptisimal kiss,*
> *ended my rebellion;*

> *my Lord is displaying His*
> *greatness as He did from*
> *earliest times;*

> *His treasuries are open,*
> *and His treasures fly out*
> *of heaven like birds,*
> *while displaying*
> *His portents in heaven;*

across the sky
these treasures form
a glorious sight;

We only have to ask for them
and our Father by His own Hand
will draw them from heaven
and place them in our heart,
so that from thereon we would be able
to express thoughts worthy of His gifts;

and I will set Knowledge in you to know Me as thrice Holy ....

30. 7. 1999

[119]have My peace and be patient, come and say:

"Father, all Merciful,
I am slow of understanding
your Divine Will;"

say it;[120]

---

[119] *Yahweh, the Father speaks.*
[120] *I said it.*

this is what I want from you:

be calm, my bride, and do not overload yourself with work; a rose has sprung in you, fresh and blooming, and while you are seated in silent meditation, contemplating Us, uniting yourself to Us, the scent of your rose fragrances Us, sending Us a most delicate scent, while We watch over you, sending Our rays in you, keeping it fresh and blooming; were you to stop contemplating Us, the loveliness of your rose will fade away .... so, your Divine Bridegroom tells you:

do not substitute your contemplation of Me with other things that withdraw you from My embrace; do not allow those who contest everything you say, My beloved, to dictate to you their whims, for I had sent you one of the noblest angels from My angelic choirs to lead you to Me; this heavenly prince withdrew you from the world, to enter, with Him, My heavenly Courts;

a human heart is too small to understand all of what I have been doing to you, especially in your so evil times where so many learned men play the sages;

I have, as I have told you, sent to you, to accompany you in your mission a prince of heaven followed with other angelic forces, as I usually do for My chosen ones; having entered into My heavenly Courts, I courted you with poetry and religion, to turn you into My harp; I have made you experience what My Gaze could give you as delights; sending It to you as a gold gleam in your eyes, filling them with My Light;

in My superabundant zeal to teach you with Wisdom, I overlooked your frailty; just as any pupil starts his school by learning the alphabet, I taught you My alphabet which is to give your whole mind to My Word;

I allowed your eyes to see My glorious Majesty; I have entrusted you with something beyond all knowledge;

be vigilant because your enemy would like to see you out of your devotion to Me and control you by overloading you with work, as a vessel when overloaded will sink; you, who are My vessel carrying My Divine Treasure, do not overload yourself lest you sink; I want to see you happy and more in contemplation of Me; your witnessing is not over; I will now let you plunge once more into My Divine Springs, granting your soul rest;[121]

ah, how could I forget the moment I approached you .... with the greatest care so as not to frighten you away I stepped by your side; and with the greatest delicacy I revealed My Love to you which until then was quite unknown to you; you had never known before of My Infinite Mercy nor the Abyss of My Love;

rejoice then, daughter, and unload your worries on Me, and let this be as a lesson to others as well, who carry more than they can carry; I do not want you to weary yourself, in order to be more productive and effectual for My Work; I said that you must not delay My Work and that you were to follow My pace alone;

all of these messages come from on high and are inspired by Me; they can profitably be used for teaching, and for refuting error; they can be used for guiding the Church into Unity and for guiding people's lives and teaching them to be holy; they are given to you for a better explanation[122] to the Revelation[123] given to you; they are an inexhaustible source of amazing grace for you all to renew you;

---

[121] *I believe too that God wants me in privacy with Him as His speech is rather personal.*
[122] *I heard at the same time 'understanding'*
[123] *The Holy Bible*

I am the Giver of Life, the Renewer of all things; I am the Source of heavenly Manna; yes, indeed! I have approached you as you were to make an amazing and prodigious union with you; unworthy you were, and far from My demand of 'equality of love', but delightful in your nothingness and your openness to My Voice;

let Me share with you; from the day you died to yourself, as a sign of My intimate friendship, I espoused you to Me, so that I have you near Me to whisper in your ear sound counsels that you may, in your turn, counsel others; I lavished you with My tenderness and My fatherly affection; with a flow of Divine Sweetness I asked you to travel with Me and for Me, from North to South and from East to West; and as I have said to you before, for your protection I have given you a multitude of angels and archangels, princes of the highest orders to accompany you in your mission, giving them orders to remain at those regions where My seeds were sown and protect what was sown;

I did not raise you in My kingly Courts, bestowing royal gifts on you for no reason; now I am taking profit from your labours and I am obtaining the delightful fruits of your labours; giving graces to My chosen ones are for various reasons: they are meant for the benefit of My people, the benefit of My Church, but at the same time for the eternal joy these chosen souls would obtain from Me in heaven;

as for those who contest each one of My Words and refuse to open their heart and see the great profit My Church obtained, refusing to see My Blessing and My Affection, they shall be judged as unworthy, since they have and are still to this day, underestimating My Power and My Mercy;

I had, Vassula, warned you never to get weary of doing good and to learn to be patient, because you would harvest in the end and at the proper time what you had sown:

- let your work be meritorious and that nothing goes in vain

- let My consolations give you courage and light in your soul

- let My fatherly affection be your constant delight in you and an intimate breeze in your soul

- let My Divine caressess be your healing balm when your soul is wounded or weary, invigorating you and effacing in you every sort of bitterness that may arise in you;

- let every spiritual exercise you do magnify in Me that you may obtain from Me boundless graces;

- let Me always be your only love and above all;

- let your mouth contain the Oil[124] given to you so that you sweetly proclaim My Greatness;

- may you appear before Me one day, perfect and honourable in My Courts ....

beloved, My Name, Yahweh, when pronounced by you, delights Me to such an extent that it makes Me incline towards you with great affection and My joy cannot be contained; the whole Court of heaven attracted by My Joy, wholeheartedly and with one voice praise My inebriated Love I have for you and for My fatherly affection; they praise Me for My Infinite Mercy I have

---

[124] *'Oil' here means 'Name', the Name of God*

for My creation;   and now let Me hear from you three 'Kyrie eleisson' ...

> *Kyrie eleisson,*
> *Kyrie eleisson,*
> *Kyrie eleisson ....*

My Mercy I give to you and My Blessings as well;   remember, do not allow yourself to be overworked;   I, God, will continue to hold you in My Power and My Grace;

Yahweh is My Name   ♡

6. 10. 1999

I lift my soul to the Lord,
to penetrate in the depths of my Father,
and taste His Sweetness;

My heart is too small though to
understand wholly the One
who encompasses all beings,
and even smaller when it tries
to understand how He who
transcends all ages and everything,
He who is sealed, and unattainable,
becomes to me unsealed and
attainable, penetrable;

in His Perfect Charity He allows me
to experience His Sweetness
by radiating in my soul His Visitation;

Most Royal Prodigy of the Prodigies,
I love you, please speak to me ....

ah, Vassula, I am invisible by essence, yet I make Myself knowable to those I choose to make Myself knowable; have you ever grasped Me by your hand?

I did ....

how have you grasped your God?

I have in a vision it pleased You
to give me, to grasp Your Hand;
Your left Hand to be more precise;
I felt Your Fingers, and Your
whole Hand is what we call:
of an aristocrat;
fine and lengthy fingers.

Then, I grasped You in another way too,
my Beloved, I grasped Your Presence,
I grasped You to possess You;
I have drawn Your Mercy
through my very wretchedness,
and You, Lover of Mankind,
Mercy beyond comprehension,
approached me, and offered Yourself to me;

yes, for you have seen Me, not with your physical eye, but with the eye of your heart, and you have grasped Me in an invisible manner ....

the Spirit who is your Teacher and your Lamp, lifts you to My Celestial Courts to contemplate what eye has not seen, and hear what ear has not heard; I am your family; so rely on My Power;

I have made you joint-heiress to Us; god by participation in the Holy Spirit; this is addressed as well to everyone, who have died to themselves and united themselves to Us, becoming in this divine union of love joint-heirs, through the Holy Spirit;

I have, as I have said many times before, in My boundless love named you Paraskevi[125] and My just herald, through grace alone; and as in the times of your ancestors, I have given you a spiritual gift, this of prophecy; I have commanded you to speak in My Name and proclaim without fear and with clarity all that I have been teaching you; I have set afire your soul to go forward and witness with ardour, enflaming other hearts to know Me; the Holy Spirit has been your remedy and the source of prophecy in these messages, but of all times too; it is He, who make you into gods by participation;

there is no better service

given to Me than this one of bringing souls back to Me; do not lack confidence because this service alone is a **divine sign** that you alone are unable to accomplish if it were not through the Holy Spirit; this is exactly how the grace of the Holy Spirit is

---

[125] *Paraskevi is a Greek name which means: 'Prepare the way to the Lord;' it means Friday.*

revealed; He alone gives you the possibilities to bring souls to Me;

I have, My so loved one, come to you repeatedly, not only as written words but as Power and as Holy Spirit in all Our Divinity, manifesting Ourselves as ever so present and as One in the Divine union of Our Oneness; when you faced great opposition all round you in Syros, have I abandoned you?[126] this made you the great example of My Power to the rest of the Cyclades; which creature could impose itself on My Holiness and on My Power?

I, Myself, have suffered by My Own countrymen,[127] so why are you surprised when you, who come from Me, suffer the same treatment? bear patiently as I bore patiently;

beloved, flesh of My Flesh, bone of My Bone, can you not see all the consolations I am giving you? My visit to you is not a day's visit; My visit to you is eternal;[128] in case you have forgotten, look again at your path My Father laid out for you: He laid out sapphire upon sapphire so that your feet walk on virtues only;

---

[126] *Syros is one island of Greece belonging to the Cyclades. I had been invited there and our Lord had opened us a wide door on the TV channel which broadcasts its program on the other 12 islands. But the Metropolitan was given orders to diffuse a pamphlet against me. Still the program went ahead with me and people liked it so much that they had to show it several times. People bought the books too.*

[127] *In records, I am inscribed that my family, from my father's side, comes from Syros.*

[128] *I had been pitying myself, for Jesus was not visiting me so often, and here was my Liturgy trying to console me with such a tender Voice, that He sounded like an unending Beatitude*

stand firm and do not falter; no man will be able to demolish My fortress;[129] I am living in this fortress and no man will be able to destroy My dwelling place; you have My word .... I will advance and you will follow; where the Spirit is, there is freedom and power;

today, the world has no eyes for heavenly things, this is why there is so much mistrust among the nations and no more freedom; the world believes in what it sees but these things last only for a time; go, My Vassula and tell this decaying world all about those things that are invisible but eternal; radiate my Glory, the light has to be placed on the roof-tops, such an overwhelming light comes only from Me; My Words given to you are a lamp for lighting a way through the dark; shine in this darkness you who carry My Word;

My brightness never fades; it is right to say that God is Fire, or when you say this is the Fire of the Holy Spirit; for you can compare it to a physical fire, which enflames everything and goes through every opening, whatever it touches it sets aflame; the Fire of God is a Fire of Love and you, My Vassula, have not been spared from it; see, how it consumes you? why, which creature, if not consumed by Love, would write prayers in religious poetry to Us?

the Holy Spirit, after branding you with His fiery baptismal kiss, setting you aflame, penetrated your intelligence, crystalizing your soul by His Divine Fire, as the rock is turned into a diamond, which is of pure carbon in crystalized form, from extreme heat; in this way too the Fire of the Holy Spirit purifies souls to become crystal clear and as pure as diamonds; this action of the Holy Spirit does not go without suffering, the one seized by those enamorous flames, suffers as he is kindled by fire, but by love

---

[129] *This sentence was pronounced like a command and with great authority. "Fortress" was meant for me.*

too; as the Fire seized you, through and through, tossing you about, transforming you from rock to diamond, the Holy Spirit in His enamoured action prepares you to see God; have you not read: "happy the pure in heart, they shall see God"? once you see God, as Scripture says, your soul will cry out:

"my Joy! how right it is to love You!"

and immediately you will seize Us to possess Us .... and I will descend from the clouds to lift you and carry you on My Wings to soar the skies; and as a tour-guide, I will tell you the history of the things that are invisible to the eye and inaccessible to the touch; I will show you My Glorious Throne from where I rule but that you too, near Me, could rule with Us ♡   **ic**

12. 2. 2000

From Your Palace, Yahweh my King,
but Father as well,
You watered me until my parched land
has had all that Your Heavens have to offer;

You use the winds as messengers
and fiery flames as servants
to proclaim to every race
Your Glory and the greatness of Your Name;

Yes! and I will continue to recite
Your marvels one by one in poetry,
for I have committed myself to You ....

[130]peace My child; all I have given you comes from Holy Wisdom; this is the way I have always worked with My prophets; I spoke and they believed; bathed constantly in My Light they dwell in My Will; knowing their human frailty, My Eyes as a mother who watch over her babe, watch over My chosen ones to keep them away from transgressing into worldly inclinations; then in My great benevolence, but with delight as well, I grant them special favours to prepare them for their task, a task that is usually beyond their human capacity; I grant them My protection, sheltering them underneath My wings,[131] and you who I have raised for a purpose and on whom I have engraved My Holy Name, I will supply you with all the needs to make the lions and the dragons roar from fear, for they will know that I Am is with you;

My all-powerful Hand does not lack means of protection, so to protect My Holy Name engraved on you now, I have you encircled with My Arms, just as one encircles his property with a fence from intruders, I have you encircled; what champion can dare come now to confront Me and challenge My choice? Prodigy Himself stooped from above to enliven this dying generation, showing My Sovereign power, but mercy as well through My Divine Work in you in a most ineffable manner; I have poured drop by drop, like distilled myrrh, My Wisdom into your ear to open your hearing;

ah,[132] what delights I gathered while performing this prodigy of prodigies! what divine pleasure I obtained from My benevolent act of Mercy, foreseeing that restoration was close at hand! what joy and gladness filled My Heart while I was freeing you from your misery and from the bondage of evil, drawing you near Me

---

[130] *Yahweh speaks*
[131] *An expression only*
[132] *God seemed delighted as He said 'ah';*

instead to become a child who will ever be at play with Me; then so as to fix your eyes on My royal dignity and that you commemorate our espousals for ever, I placed the sweetest kisses upon those lips which would glorify My Name, increasing your attention on My supreme sweetness, and so that I hear you say: "the Lord God has espoused me, adorning my soul with Himself, oh how very pleasng it is to our Lord when a soul is supple and willing, for His impenetrable Wisdom will find its way in her[133] and draw her ever completely in Him;"

Scriptures say: "happy the man whom You choose, whom You invite to live in Your courts;"[134] yes, happy is he, for I fill My chosen one with good things of My House and these good things are holy instructions coming from My Mouth; I then adorn My prophet with celestial riches and splendour which are the virtues;

My temple I want holy and pure, My altar I want unblemished and sparkling like a thousand gems; I turn his tongue like a double-edged sword to go out and speak against all pride and arrogance, against all the lofty speakers, against all human pride, against all that is highly thought of by men, against injustice and against all that contradicts My Law of Love;

I take pleasure in My dwelling place[135] for My Spirit rests on him who is to borne My Word; wedded with the Truth, My prophet is sent out as My royal ambassador in every vile corner of this earth to hymn to you: righteousness, kindness, holiness, virtue and reminding all of you of My Ways; reminding every man from all ranks that:

---

[133] *the soul*
[134] *Ps 65 : 4*
[135] *"dwelling place" is used instead of the word 'prophet';*

- Unction of the poor in spirit, I Am;

- Guarantor of your well-being, I Am;

- Luminous Godhead and Source of Sublime Love, I Am;

- Sovereign and Bridegroom of all creation, I Am;

- Restorer and Lamp of body and soul, I Am;

- Consoler of the persecuted in the cause of right, I Am;

- Balm and Ointment of the sick and the dying, I Am; and that I am your Lord and God but your Friend, your Companion and your Father as well;

I am, generation, ceaselessly giving Myself to you, to perfect your image which you have so deformed and sullied by all your evil doings, your sins and your obstinate resistance to acknowledge Me as your Father; and if I am ceaselessly giving Myself to you, it is so as to elevate you by grace and that through grace your sight may be restored to see the invisible things that never wear out; this is why I am raising prophets in My good Will with one utterance from My Mouth to join them to My Heart;

I, the Luminous Godhead had anticipated long before your creation this Great Apostasy; have I no right then to raise prophets? all heaven rejoices since in Our gracious condescension We took pity on your apathy; I have raised prophets to receive directly and at all times My celestial calls accompanied by a flow of graces ♡ I share with them, in the proximity of their heart, all My Divine Works; I have and am, breathing inspirations from My Heart in their heart so that they faithfully testify; and if I scandalize through them many haughty people, it is because their [136]ways are not My ways;

through My zeal for saving this generation, I have raised prophets and espoused them to Me; I taught them how to spend their time with Me, and how to share their life with Me while still on earth, according to the grace I have given them;

in these days I am descending together with My Son and My Holy Spirit as three Witnessess; I am Spirit,[137] in that I send My Holy Spirit of Truth[138] to be with you forever and lead you to the complete Truth; think of My Mercy and worship Me;

the Word[139] was with Me and He existed since the beginning; He who is nearest to My Heart has witnessed and made Me known to you; My Word testifies on earth as I and the Holy Spirit testify; My Son, Jesus Christ, who bought His Church with His Own Blood testifies with His Blood[140] and the Holy Spirit who leads you to the complete Truth[141] testifies with Water;[142] in all We are

---

[136] *the haughty people*

[137] *Jn 4 : 24. St. Paul too in 1 Cor 15 : 45 speaks of Christ as "life-giving Spirit". The description "Spirit" in the biblical sense does not define God's nature so much as it describes His life-giving activity. God is Spirit in that He gives the Spirit.*

[138] *Jn 14 : 17*

[139] *Jesus Christ*

[140] *With His Sacrifice we obtained Eternal Life.*

[141] *Jn 16 : 12-13: Jesus says: "I still have many things to say to you but they would be too much for you now; but when the Spirit of Truth comes He will lead you to the complete Truth ..." It is a mistake to speak of an end to Revelation and treat it as a deposit of sentences. God is active and alive and will continue to show Himself through the Holy Spirit, never stopping in doing so. When one says in Latin, "complere", it means that Christ is the full, complete revelation of God; and not that He will stop revealing Himself to mankind. The Holy Bible is the narrative testimony of Jesus Christ. It is NOT God's last word.*

three Witnessess and all three of Us agree as We are One God alone,[143] with one Will, one Power and one Dominion; and you can attribute the Power, the Holy Wisdom and the Infinite Goodness to all three of Us;

Love compels Me to grant you, generation, the spirit of prophecy to some so that they carry out what I order them to do; they are fed with mouthfuls of honey[144] and oil[145] to proclaim the greatness of My Name; to keep them founded in the Truth and on intelligent reflection, I have many a time rebuked, corrected and taught them so that they become an unction to those I bring back into My House; I have instructed them with Holy Wisdom and Wisdom is entirely constituted by the fulfilling of the Law;

I have taught My prophets to contemplate Me in My Holiness allowing them and giving them access to My Nobility to rejoice in My direct Presence and taste My sweetness ♡ therefore, the only theology, and I would strongly add, the only **true** theology is the contemplation of Me, your God, and a foretaste of the Beatific Vision; this is the true and holy theology; it is not the learned theologian who shifts his papers with his theology that turns him into a prophet to prophesy, but those I, Myself, anointed with the unction of My Love, embedding them well within My Heart to reach the interiour Divine and extraordinary inspirations that lie in My Heart, to be pronounced like fire to My people;

ah, Vassula, and how many times I heard from the earth a trickling of amused laughter and arrogance, accompanied by complete resentment and deafness as well, when you correct them

---

[142] *With Baptism*
[143] *In the unity of essence*
[144] *honey: represents Celestial Manna, the Word of God.*
[145] *oil: represents the Name of God (Sg 1 : 3)*

in My Name! yes, the sinners wave reproof aside, finding all sorts of excuses to do what they want;

I manifest, in a most ineffable manner, Myself to My prophets, yes, while they are still here on earth and they are aware of this grace; I array them with Myself, I array their nakedness, adorning them with Myself and they know it, they are conscious of My Divine Presence during contemplation;

I have anointed you to draw from My Heart all the divine inspirations for every need, to be given to My people as an unction and as a refreshing morning dew on a parched land; I have taught you by grace as well how to interpret My desires; I have said throughout this Divine Revelation, but as well as in former Revelations, that I, Myself, instruct My chosen ones, and I become their spiritual director, to teach them the way to go; I, for My part, celebrate My benevolence for bringing rescue to those I love and they, in turn, sing for joy the psalms of David in the shadow of My wings;

You crown those You love with Your bounty,
abundance of graces cover their heads;
Your cup overflows while You share it,
You immortalize them with Your Name,
You dress their soul with brocades of virtues;
so that Your Kingly Heart
falls in love with their beauty;

yes, tell this lethargic generation that God is here; My Works are sublime and those who have recognized My Voice in these messages are blessed; those who delight in them are right to fix their eyes on them, because every Work coming out of My Merciful Hand is full of glory and majesty; I remind My people that prophecy is alive, since it comes from My Power that I wield, so why this arrogance from the nations? have you not heard that I personally pay them tribute with My direct intervention?

yes, indeed! and I hold them close to My Heart, as a mother holds preciously her child on her heart; in this manner too I hold My prophets close to My Heart and woe! woe to anyone who would dare stretch out their hand and try to touch them without My Authority!

be happy, Vassiliki, for My allowing you to walk in and out, and freely too, in My Heavenly Courts; may your soul rejoice in My Mercy; the Church is pining away in its great apostasy, an apostasy foretold but kept secret; was I then to remain silent too?

I will not keep silent as the devil wishes, no, but I will keep raising prophets to announce and denounce, to shine like a lamp where there is darkness; I teach them to be generous and gratify Me by lavishly responding to My Call while held in thought and contemplation in My enamoured Arms; I fill their mouth with worship and their spirit with joy; as the blood runs in one's veins continuously with no exteriour sound, so has My Holy Spirit, in this tranquil manner been teaching you, Vassula, with Wisdom, for your salvation and for those of others, and if I happened to admonish you now and then, it was for your spiritual growth and your own progress;

I had, since all eternity, foreseen this apostasy in the Church as well, but I had also foreseen My Salvific Plan in you, where I would descend from My Throne and address you in divine poetry My Love Theme and reveal to you and through you to others My loving intercession through My Infinite Mercy;

you lacked, generation, and I came to fill you, but you are not happy, because to this very day I am speaking, you are resenting

My teachings; I came to heal your apostasy, and the contrite hearts heard Me; I came to raise your dead to get to know Me as their Father, through My Holy Spirit, and it is only through Him that Divine Knowledge can be obtained and disclosed to those We have chosen, since they have the Holy Spirit Himself as their Counselor and Educator; for through Him and not through human knowledge are they[146] given the grace into their intellect to perceive the Triune God and speak with Him; no adroit sort of cleverness coming from human reasoning can tell them they have not met Me; it is as though you would be telling them, 'you are naked', when they know they are dressed; I Myself have adorned them with Myself; but the devil took the best out of My dignitaries in the Church and held you responsible for doctrinal errors, whereas My repeated inspirations to you through the Holy Spirit should have made it clear to them, and they would have understood that it was a vehement temptation from the evil one;

Satan, jealous of all the gifts I am pouring out on this dying generation to save it, jealous of you, whom I have chosen, still dripping with heavenly dew from My Courts where you have been raised up to send out as My precious gift to all nations, enraged, and swore in his jealousy to destroy you by vomiting his venom over you to appear detestable, deformed, dangerous and ugly; but your Blessed Mother ran to your rescue and covered you with Her Mantle;

by grace I have raised you to call Me when you wished, a unique imperial gift that I seldom give to My chosen ones;[147] but Satan again in his jealousy drew many to ridicule you, while drawing them on his side; in spite of the good fruits I have amassed to

---

[146] *The prophets*
[147] *Our Lord, from the beginning told me that I could call Him whenever I wished and He would reply always. And so He has, ever since, replied whenever I called to Him.*

offer them, even so, they went on challenging Me, rebelliously disregarding My fruits and My counsel,[148] and remain as perverse and disloyal as their ancestors' sons, provoking Me with their high places;

then there are some who believed that I spoke, but even to those Satan gave a spirit of lethargy, a human adaptability to My Prodigies, in which with time, this spirit makes them lose their interest in My Prodigies, Prodigies that are a life-giving fountain, and which can lead them to Eternal Life;

you must have heard the parable of the sower; "when anyone hears the word of the kingdom without understanding, the evil one comes and carries off what was sown in his heart;" these people stand inert, stupefied, uncomprehending;

then you have those who raised a whole jubilee upon hearing through My messenger the echo of My Voice, welcoming My prophet with great joy, storming the other cities to announce that the word of the kingdom is being addressed to them anew, freely, and with power; but this enthusiasm quickly died out because in their heart, My word had found only patches of rock, and made no roots in them; with the first persecution on account of My word, or even a small trial coming their way, they could not last; no, they are not the ones who, when people will abuse them and speak all kinds of evils and calumny against them on account of My Name would stand firm, since they never had any solid foundation; they will be the first to fall;

Sovereignty was not understood and was rejected .... and My ambassadors[149] of peace weep bitterly over their parched hearts;

---

[148] *One can tell them by their fruits*
[149] *the prophets*

Satan has sent his rage as well as he could, to destroy My gift[150] to mankind; ploughmen, to set to work on your back, My Vassula, making furrows to break you; but My right Hand shattered their yoke into smithereens;

but listen to this, Vassula, I have brought your whole family out of the land of the blessed land of Egypt, where to this day the perfume of My Son, His Mother and Joseph the Just, still rises from that land all the way to heaven; already there I welcomed you, and swore an oath: "through this flower I will gather you together from different nations and different creeds and reveal to all of you My Fatherly Love and Mercy; through her frailty I will raise nations, renewing them by a spiritual revolution; I intend, through this flower to display My Holiness for all the nations to see; and for those who give orders to My prophets not to prophesy, I will give a prodigious prophetic Call and an Order from My Throne on My Choice, anointing her so that she would not resist My Prophetic Call;"

Egypt! I raised a prophet from your land; you gave bread to My Son, so why should I not raise a prophet from you? from this prophet will issue My Word until the horns of the evil ones are revealed and exposed;

when I speak, who can refuse to prophesy?[151] do two friends take the road together if they had not planned to do so?[152] no more do I do anything without revealing My Plans to My prophets ♡[153] and so I have with you, Vassula, revealed not only My Plans but My Holy Countenance as well; and all I foretold has come true at the appropriate time; the Word of Life was given to you freely to

---

[150] *God means, me.*
[151] *Am 3 : 8*
[152] *Am 3 : 3*
[153] *Am 3 : 7*

adopt you and make you god by participation; but Satan again will visit the minds of My people, knowing their ignorance, to bring them to temptation to cast stones at you for My expression;

ah, if only the world would come to peace terms with My Triune Holiness, they would understand My sayings!

I promise you, and this is your Father in Heaven speaking to you, the One who you said once of Him: "my Father in Heaven, I know, has a weakness for me, but I too have a weakness for Him;" says to you, burning with Divine Love: "I will continue to cover you with My Sweetness, graciously deploying in you, giving Myself more to you, and filling your soul like a sweet substance so that you in your turn would give more of yourself to Me, becoming in this way one spirit with Me, one spirit with the Divine; then I will once more send you out to the nations, as My adorned gift, to instruct them with kindness, drawing them to Us into a filial love, expanding their heart to receive more of Us and all that is Divine; then in this tranquility which I will bring their soul, they will suddenly see everything in Our Light, overpowering Satan's temptations; from thereon they too will be called 'gods by participation' and they will rule with Us;"

now, I have granted you and through you to others to understand your position; **I restore nations through the sufferings and sacrifices of those whom I have chosen**, although often they come to Me lamenting that they feel they have toiled in vain, and have exhausted themselves for nothing; they have done all that was ordered for them to do, glorifying Me, for they have been under My observance permanently, during their contemplation;

this true theology which lifts the soul, soaring up in the third Heaven, giving them a foretaste of the Beatific Vision, during which, in a supernatural way, I speak to them, honouring them to see their inheritance and the inheritance of all the saints; and while they are reposing in My Arms I bless them, invigorating My Fire within them to go out with zeal and without fear to proclaim My Word; ♡

Blessed is God and His Holy Name
for He reveals with bounty His intentions
to the winds who are His messengers;
wrapped in a robe of light,
His Majesty reveals to them His prowess;

I call in my wretchedness to my God thrice Holy
and like a gust of wind coming from nowhere
He flowers me while descending on me;
and I, like an opened flower absorb His Divine Light;

*God has sung to me and to **all** of you*
dear brothers and sisters!
The One who is enthroned on the cherubs
has revealed His Mercy to us;
no one can say: "I have not seen
the saving power of our God in my house,"
for in His Presence are splendour and majesty;
for He comes, He comes to you all
not to judge you, not yet, but to deify you;

are you happy, Vassula?

I am, more than happy;
You planted me in Your House
and I flourished in Your Courts,
so that I proclaim Your Greatness,
so how could I not be happy in Your Arms?
no one will rob me of my happiness,

no persecution, no abuse, no calumny, no insult
and not even all hell thrown on me
to tear me to pieces can rob me of the
happiness You gave me and continue to give me;
so let this earth learn who is God,
and praise His Name;

ah, blessed be Your Name, for ever!

and I will tell you this: I swore an oath to you on My Mercy and on My Faithfulness; so I will continue to uphold you in My right Hand, giving you with My Presence an unbounded joy and a foretaste of the Beatific Vision; and I will continue being your Counsellor and your happiness, My child; ravines may fold upon you and black clouds cover you, and clods of earth may cover you, but I assure you, you will go by unscathed, and My Light upon you will radiate even more powerfully;

be soothed with My Oil; I am determined to save this generation by parading My Mercy; so be happy all you who hear the melody of My Voice and have your fill in Me, your God;

8. 3. 2000

Bodyguard of my soul
You have sprinkled my soul with myrrh,
and covered my head with sweetly
scented perfumes, by Your Presence;
and now, I am again with You,
Your closeness to You is wealth
for my soul, my mind and my heart;
Your closeness to Your royal Munificence
renders me strong and eager,
eager to reach an invincible holiness ....

I love you; even in such wretchedness I can obtain My joy and My Word can abide in you through My transcendence; I am not speaking only for you and for this generation, but I am putting all of this on record also for the next generation, so that a race to be born can praise Me, your God; look how I am now leaning down from the heights of My Sanctuary ....

ah, Vassula, Heaven has never leaned down so close to the earth as it is leaning now; some time ago I could hear from earth a sigh or two, but now, I hardly hear anything; this is why I am moved to pity you, generation;

what I hear from the corpse in a bragging tone is: "look! I can live in a desert like the pelican; I can live in a ruin like the screech owl; I can live without God for I can do better than God ...."

I then turn My Eyes the other way and look at My Own household and see haughty looks, proud hearts, mistrust, slander, cardinal against cardinal, bishop against bishop ....

Lord! are You telling me that
Your Hand is too short now to redeem?
Have You suddenly not the Strength to save?
You are known to be slow to anger,
but not slow to intervene and save!
So why do You wait?
Why are You not intervening? now!

do you dare challenge My Wisdom? are you provoking My Omnipotence?

ah, Lord, to compose Your Household,
I can give my life for it and I have given it;
but my zeal for Your House devours me,
and when it comes to lift Your House
so that it does not fall,
I have given my soul and body,
regardless of the consequences;
I have sweated blood,
and at times spat out blood from the
scourge that crushed me,
and You know it;

I was handed down by Your Own
after they had hounded me like game;
but no complaint was heard from me;
For no reason they treated me as a renegade,
but I withstood all the trials I faced,
for Your mighty Hand withheld my frailty;

my days are swirling like dust
to return to dust,
and I see no end to Your Holy Agony;
so for how long yet am I to keep saying:

*"too long am I to live among
people who hate peace?"*

*for how long am I to watch
heaven mourning for its
household and its holy City?*

*am I to remain passive while You are
being recrucified unnecessarily?*

*You know me my Lord,
You who turned me like a sycamore
from Egypt, that I would go,
had I even to crawl, in every country
as You command,
and grain everywhere
Your Word given to me, even on
the mountain tops,
I would go, and down to the ravines;*

*You know me Lord,
my mouth would not want for
arguments with Your Wisdom,
nor Your Omnipotence; never!*

*but the pillars of heaven tremble
struck with awe from all that they
see in Your House;*

*the angels tremble on the
tremendous scourge that is awaiting
us in the coming days;
so how could I compose myself in chaos?*

Vassula, I shall tell you something in a few moments, something you do not know, but let Me tell you already this:

I am going to do something[154] in your own days that you would not believe if you were to be told of it .... then, this is what you should know: I have in this very Household I have been telling you about, kept a tiny remnant for Myself, chosen by grace, nothing to do with their good deeds; they are: a whispered echo of My Voice; am I not likely to hear these whispered cries?

(I looked sideways at Jesus and said:)

have I set my face for a moment against You like flint?

I have given you birth, I have opened the eye of your intellect to understand Me, see Me and see all the invisible things; I have opened your ear with drops of myrrh to listen like a disciple and I provided you with speech; I have set your feet on the way I wanted you to go, accompanied by a prince from the highest order of Archangels; I offered you drink from My Cup, so, will My Hand deal with you harshly? you have offered Me your life as an atonement for the rebellion and the division of My Church;

---

[154] *(From that date which the message was being received, 8.3.00, in less than two weeks, while on a pilgrimage and gathering of the TLIG family in the Holy Land; we were given permission by the Greek Orthodox Patriarchate of Jerusalem to celebrate 2 Orthodox Liturgies with pre-sanctified gifts, in the Holy Sepulchre Church and on Mount Tabor, and invite everyone to receive the Holy Communion; we were 450 people with 12 Church denominations and there were no restrictions or interdiction to receive Holy Communion)*
– I think, maybe it was the 1ˢᵗ time in history, after the great Schism that the Greek Orthodox, invited EVERYONE to receive the Holy Blood and Body of Christ. Yes, indeed, Jesus I would not have believed if I were to be told of before this happened! Glory be to God!)

I have been touched by your zeal and your concern for My Household; I am pleased that I have not heard you say instead:

"leave that place, for Your Eyes are too pure to see what you see, leave them at their fate and touch nothing unclean over there ...."

- I was simply lost in amazement over your courage, but I had brought fire out of you; I opened your mouth ....

beloved, I once said to you, that any delicacy from the part of My creatures to restore My tottering House, touches Me profoundly, I have not, My Vassula, appointed you only as My just herald but as My sentry as well over the House of the West;

when you hear a word of My Mouth given to you, you are, bound to your vows of fidelity with Me, obliged to pass on to those I am sending you, My word of warning; if you would refuse to pass on My word to them, I would hold you responsible;

- if, however, you pass on My word to them and they do not repent, they will die for their sin, but you yourself will go by unscathed and you shall not be held responsible nor will you die;

I have not only appointed you as an intercessor to the House of the East but to the House of the West, too; when you hear Me blazing with wrath for their rigidity which keeps them separated and therefore in sin, you are to intercede for them as you did;

My Royal Authority will then deal gently with My Household; but as for the proud who would not repent, I will pluck them up by the roots and in their place I will plant the lowly; I am known

117

to overthrow the proud; pride was not born of Me but of the devil ....

so, **be rich in poverty** ♡ and water this arid land with My prophecies to you; he who waters will be watered by the King Himself; then the King Himself will pay you tribute and will address you in poetry and hymn; He will fill your mouth with honey and you shall speak for Him to the nations;

I will be gracious to you, giving you more of My friendship to you; be happy, daughter; your King has favoured you and dressed you in brocades, perfuming you in His Presence, while myrrh wafts from His robes; He has allowed you in His palace and given you access in His nuptial chamber; I tell you, daughter: in My Household I will advance My step with you; I and you together, with all sorts of princes of the highest ranks from heaven in our train and we will enter in My Sanctuary, while My Presence will come upon them like dawn; so do not fumble with the sickle but hold it firmly and with a good grip too and reap, Vassiliki, reap! reap where My angels' fingers point for you to reap and you will reap the reward of virtue ♡

give to your King as much as He has given you ....

I am only a puff of wind,
how am I to give You as much as
You have given me?
You have given me Life!

I will never, ever, ever, never ever,
be able to give You as much as
an inkling of what You have, in Your
gracious condescension, given me!

I know .... but give Me as much as your means can afford; empty yourself of all that comes from Me and is good and offer it to Me;

(I understood then that our Lord was not only asking me to offer my services to Him alone but to be available as well, reaching others and coming out of my way, to be at the service of mankind and help them as much as I can. To serve the 'neighbour', practice virtue and keep nothing for myself.)

yes, give! give to those who wait from you and bear witness on My Good Works and I will be with you; and as My Father said to you sometime ago, I tell you the same thing: "ravines may fold upon you and black clouds cover you, and clods of earth may cover you, but I assure you, I will be with you and you will go by unscathed;" remember: there is no frontier between you and Me; I am always with you, My loved one; ♡ **ic**

24. 4. 2000

Have mercy Lord on this
unfaithful generation of
which I also make part of it!

rouse My child and trust Me; have I not shown you My glory and what is in store for the people I love while in the Holy Land?

listen, a man was known to have to keep blowing a furnace to produce any heat, and the sun is known to burn the mountains three times as much, but when My Spirit who is pure fire, emerges from above, He is known to consume and put aflame everything He touches in no time at all, for who was known to have withstood His blaze? and He puts aflame everyone who loves Him, turning them into living torches so that their words may flare in the night of your dark generation; and like a torch in the darkness they will flare My Words;

"creation!" they will cry out, "set out to find your Husband[155] again!" they will flare My Words which will overturn the heresies and anything that is pervert; in My Name they[156] will combat the forked weapons;[157] I mean to cultivate this society and make them understand that immortality is found in being kin to Our Triune Holiness; Our Royal Munificence will keep those chosen souls perseverant;

I am now to share with you My joy; ah, Vassula, I have observed him and what I saw pleased Me; I have consecrated him with royal prodigality and I have anointed him to preside over worship and teach My House My decrees and enlighten the land he lives in, on My Law, which is based on Love; although there will be those who will join forces against him, he himself shall go by unscathed; there will be jealous men who will hound him, but I will be on his side;[158]

I refreshed you all,[159] have I not? I have granted you special favours, have I not? ah, Vassula, My Holy Countenance shall never dissipate from your heart for I have it engraved in you; I transcend earth and heaven in majesty and splendour so never get daunted, since I am the Ultimate and Unfathomable Wisdom,

---

[155] *God: "For now your Creator will be your Husband ..."(Is 54 : 5)*
[156] *Our Lord is speaking of the apostles of the end of times;*
[157] *I understood by 'forked weapons': the devil and his demons;*
[158] *Jesus was speaking about a Greek Orthodox priest who delighted Him, nevertheless, Jesus already announced that his mission will not go by without persecution, but Jesus will be on his side.*
[159] *While in the Holy Land. We were 450 pilgrims, family of TLIG, with 12 Church denominations;*

count on My Wisdom and remember: I have put by your side more than one heavenly prince,[160] and, My Vassula, through your weakness I will bring forth unity; and you who read Me, I tell you, remain straight in Holy Wisdom and upright, then you will do My Will; you will only have to say: "yes!" and I will bring you immediately in union with Our Oneness and fill you with My Transcendent Light so that you will be filled with the absolute fullness of Our Triune Deity to understand as well that the nobility of unity will be when you too will incline your head in humility, love and self-effacement;

the humble man's prayer pierces the clouds, Scriptures say,[161] but it also pierces the dungeons of the evil one and shatters his plans ♡ the humble man's prayers have a double effect to My benefit; if people, My Vassula, ask you again: "what does our Lord say in His most recent messages?" tell them: "the Lord, my God, says nothing new, so continue to keep firm and immovable in your faith; as for those who are still asleep, our Saviour, Jesus Christ says to them: 'wake up from your stupor as you should and leave sin alone;' God called you too and to this day you have not heard Him; you are rejecting His Triune Holiness and you are rejecting Him who gives you His Holy Spirit; if you belong to the Light, then you belong to the day and in the day you should remain awake; but if you ask: 'what does our Lord say in His most recent Message?' it is because you are still not rooted in Him who created you and you still have not understood Him; you have no understanding of Him, your God;

ah, if you knew what spells lie in His Love! and what enchanting treasures lie in His Sacred Heart! He has, since you were born, been calling you; how much longer are you going to go astray?

---

[160] *Christ means, angels ...*
[161] *Si 35 : 17*

121

did you not know that under His Eyes you will find true peace? so you who dwell in the desert, do not despair; the Lover of mankind, our Lord God and all, is near you now to fetch you and take you in His House and into His private room[162] where He will seal your heart with His Divine Kisses; then, everyone who will see you will call you, 'betrothed of the Holy One' upon Whom all authority was given;

and as for your own friends, they will question themselves upon seeing you coming up from the desert, "who is this one coming up from the desert leaning on a column of pure incense whose fragrance is spreading over us and in the breeze?" then, enflamed with pure love, you will respond, "like cinnamon and acanthus, I have in the Holy Spirit, yielded a perfume, like choice myrrh, in Him and through Him, I have breathed out a scent; I have been transfigured in my Creator's Divine Love!"

"but who was He on whom you leaned?" "He? He is the Alfa and the Omega, the Lover of mankind who draws every soul to Himself to follow Him; do you not see? I had once been when you knew me, like our ancestors in the desert, and like them I was following Futility becoming futile myself; now, Spring Himself visited me and flowered me; He fragranced me and adorned my soul with wreathes of gardenias; He blessed my soul in His Name thrice holy, and now, I too can say: 'I have an understanding of God, whose Love is like a flash of fire; I am now a child of God, why, I am on my way to be deified for having accepted our Father and made peace with Him .... ah, how I delight! for I have no frontiers now with my Creator; no, none at all, no more frontiers!"

---

[162] *I understood by this, that the private room is our Lord's Heart.*

hence even the utmost wretched will have a Divine Visitation, for My Return is imminent; I will visit those who are not even familiar with My Divine Works; in their nothingness they have acquired nothing and have no knowledge of Me, nor have they ever known that I Am who I Am is their Master and God .... in your days when evil and wickedness are inhaled daily by this generation, My great Love compels Me to stoop down from My Throne and open the reserves of graces in Heaven to pour them unmeritedly upon this generation and save it; you may call it: a period of unlimited graces; I am He, who so lavishly sends the Holy Spirit to you, and I am not doing this because of your merits, but I am doing it because of the ineffable condescension of My Love;

I will keep flooding you, generation, in your chaos, with unmerited graces, immersing you to raise you all to such nobility that when the moment comes to present you to the Father, your soul will appear gleaming gold, for I would have clothed you with Myself;

listen to Daniel your guardian angel to what he has to say as a witness: "in your earthly state you will not be received in front of God's Throne, no one has been received in that state, but you will be received by God, to enter Heaven, only when Christ will be your garment; only then God will recognize you ...."

yes, this is why I will keep giving Myself continuously to you, giving you more of Myself to you and manifesting Myself to you in power and grace while I will be visiting you, adorning thus your soul with majesty and prodigality; I will, at the same time, be embellishing you, adorning you as a bride is adorned for her marriage by divine grace and virtue while My Mouth will be hymning to you Instruction in poetry, clothing you in Wisdom and Knowledge of Myself, honouring Us in Our Triune Holiness;

the King, in His graciousness will saturate your soul to lift you from the prison of your flesh and enter into My Sublime Light, a Light ten thousand times brighter than the sun; approach Me then, you who would like to be deified and enter into the joy of Our Triune Holiness to become, in our Divine Union, gods by participation ....

and you, who make My Heart desire you all the more in your ineffable weakness, My Vassula, I tell you: be one with Me, let My protective Hand guide you ♡ let Me always be your sole Joy, the Sunshine of your soul, the gleaming Path of your life, the Enlightenment of your decisions; My Eyes are upon you, you can say, fixed on you;

remember, beloved, when you are thirsty, come, little one, to Me, your Bridegroom, I will always have drink to give you; do not listen to the hisses, nor to the vipers' tongues; the Holy Spirit has marked you with His Holy Seal and befriended you, marking you as Ours; come and enjoy a period of rest in Us; and if a passer-by asks you: "where is your rest?" reply and say: "my rest is in the Heart of Jesus Christ, the One who is nearest to the Father's Heart" ♡

ΙΧΘΥΣ

28. 4. 2000

Orthodox Calendar: *Good Friday –*

my Lord, my Resurrection,
my Blessedness,
I lack nothing in Your Holy Presence,
Lord, You open Your Mouth
to speak to me
and Light inundates me from Your Mouth;
my Liturgy, my Litany, the Light of Wisdom,
behold, stands before me;

Today again, is the day
when innocent Blood
was shed for my sake,
and while Satan is spitting out his venom
on Your Holy Name,
I come to You, to console You
and adore You;

ah, Lamb of God, you have not
overthrown your scourgers,
nor ordered them to lay the scourge aside,
You have not opened Your Mouth to plead:
"I am worn out with the blows you deal me;"
but remained silent towards Your tormentors;
because Your Heart was smouldering with Passion;
You remained silent,
You remained silent so as
not to aggravate Your Angels,
already distressed;

My friends and My companions shrank away from My Wounds and even the dearest ones kept their distance ....

they had abandoned Me ....

even to steady My step and keep Me from falling, while I was carrying My Cross, they were not there; My Heart was throbbing and My strength deserting Me; the light of My Eyes diminishing, while violent men were attacking Me, ranting in their speech with swords on their lips, My Heart writhed within Me; I could have asked the Angels to give Me wings like a dove, to fly away and find rest, and find a refuge from the storm of abuse, but I had answered when My Father called Me;

Your Father heard Your plea and
ransomed You and gave You His Peace,
from the feud against You;

Lying witnesses had taken their stand,
yet You wept when they were sick and dying;
like someone mourning his mother,
You wept for them;

Shame and dishonour was not of Your
concern, facing the Cross;
but in the face of Your tormentors,
You cried out once more to the Father;
'Eli, Eli, Lama sabachthani?'
but the Father's attention was turned on us,
and saw all the human race, and pitied us ...
so once more Your Father denied
what Your lips were entreating Him
as He had denied Your supplication
in Gethsemane;

Yahweh had leaned down from the heights of His Sanctuary and looking down on the earth, He heard the sighing of the captive and to set free those doomed to die,

He sacrificed His only Begotten Son ....

yes, indeed, My Father gave Me to all of you as a gift for your redemption with My entire Will too;

> *yet, Holy One, You who are one*
> *in the Father and the Father is one*
> *in You, You, for my sake, preferred*
> *to become on the Cross,*
> *the scorn of the men who surrounded You*
> *and the jest of Your people;*
> *I AKRA TAPINOSI*[163]

"let Yahweh save Him", they said; "if Yahweh is His friend let Him rescue Him!" but I heard nothing, as though I were deaf, as though dumb, saying not a word; I was like the one who, hearing nothing, has no sharp answer to make ♡ My strength was trickling away from Me, the light had gone away from My Eyes,

> *ah Lord, when we stumble,*
> *Your Powerful Hand is there to save us,*
> *but, You, on the way to the Crucifixion, when You*
> *stumbled, the crowd gathered in glee, gathered around You;*
> *strangers You never even knew tore You apart incessantly;*
> *when You made Your first fall, they surrounded You,*
> *grinding their teeth at You,*
> *thinking You had already given up Your Spirit*
> *and would not make it for the Crucifixion;*

---

[163] *Greek: the ultimate humility*

the earth quivered and quaked; the foundations of the mountains trembled;

"I will not break My Covenant;
I will not revoke My given Word;
I have sworn on My Holiness,
once for all .... My dynasty
shall last forever;"

then the Anointed One gave up His Spirit ...

*There is a River[164] whose streams
sanctify the dwelling[165] of the Most High;*

and when God is in the city,[166] it cannot fall; today, in this hour of crisis, when the devil gathered all his evil dominion against you, pouring out his contempt upon the nobly born, I, in My turn call out My chosen ones, as it was My purpose to continue expanding My Church and progressing it, to bring within it many of My children into glory, it seemed to Me right to go through sufferings and become the prototype example for those who would follow Me in the future and become the bone of My Bone, the flesh of My Flesh and continue atoning for their brothers and sisters;

I have never ceased appointing prophets, setting them in the way of the Truth for My Salvific Plan; I bring them to fulfil their noble vows that had risen to their lips at our Divine enamoured encounter; when they allowed, in their great love for Me, and their noble conviction to be committed in My Salvific Plan, I stepped forward, and with My Royal Sceptre, I branded them

---

[164] *River: Holy Spirit*
[165] *dwelling: God lives in us*
[166] *city: we are God's city*

with the same marks I, Myself, was branded, to resemble Me and turn them into My likeness ♡

all those who truly accepted Me are not ashamed of Me; nor are they ashamed of those celestial marks showing that they do not belong to the world anymore; today you will recognize them by the zeal they have for My House, My House that dresses them, a zeal that devours them; you will recognize them when you see them putting up with insults for My Sake, calumny, spittle and persecution; yes, for My Sake they will allow themselves to be dragged in mire and constantly threatened; they will not hide their face from trouble but they will endure with peace all the trials and their hearts shall not be broken but sanctified; nor will they break their vow of fidelity of sharing My Cross;

so if you happen to notice their wounds and you ask them:

"who has made those wounds on you?" they will all tell you:

"I have offered my back to atone for you; these wounds you see I have received with savagery in the house of my Master's friends .... it is because I have been telling them the truth that they made me an enemy and treated me as such; they want to escape persecution for the Cross of our Saviour by not keeping the Law of Love; but it does not matter and I give no attention to my wounds because what is important to me it is to know about the Cross, the Instrument of our redemption; the Cross of our Redeemer, through whom the world is crucified to me now and I to the world;[167] obedience to God comes before obedience to men, say the Scriptures[168] and so I have obeyed and followed the heavenly instructions given to me;"

---

[167] *Gal 6 : 14*
[168] *Acts 5 : 29*

"what did you say when they descended on you as conquerors, those very ones who wounded you and who say are friends to your Master?"

"I have never asked myself why has this happened to me, because I made an oath to our God and Redeemer, signing it with my own blood to become the slave of our Saviour;"

"and what does your Divine Master say to all of this?"

"He who encompasses all beings without being contained by their limits is in mourning for His Household; many of His shepherds have laid His House waste; in their rebellion they have trampled down His Rules and have turned His glorious pastures into a desolation; their entire vineyard is ravaged as well; and the flock finding only barren lands and nothing to graze on, depraved, they died,[169] and they together with them died as well .... these things are happening and none of these seem to take it to heart; they have been assailed by their human rules and have failed Him;"

"how do you know of so many things and see them?"

"it is only through the Light of the Cross that one can perceive those things that are invisible to the eye; it is through the Eye of our Redemptive Instrument and of our Salvation that one sees all its bearings; but when it comes to know about these things, only through a joined divine union with Christ, being one with Him can one know from His Own Mouth of these things, and if one accepts to be marked as 'Slave of Christ'; yes, accepting divine slavery; one's heart then is not only grafted on Jesus' Divine Heart, but it is grafted as well on His Cross with all the bearings it could offer; they could be sorrows, but delights too; I am

---

[169] *spiritually*

convinced that I belong to Christ and to the Holy Cross, for He has said so ....

our Divine Master but Bridegroom too, plants us in His Heart and when we take root and flourish within His Heart, we bear ample and good fruit; we have become heirs to His Kingdom and gods by participation, his adoptive children;

God does not deprive me of Knowledge, but speaks to me in plain words, face to face, and His Voice is music to my ears, addressing me with majestic power His thoughts, He enlightens my intellect to understand the hidden sense of proverbs and in His smiles and delight He unseals mysterious sayings of Scriptures that were kept hidden from our eyes;

yes, there is a proper time for everything He does; my Lord and my God has sealed me with divine kisses, He has sealed my soul with the imprint of His Triune Holiness so as to draw me even more into the fullness of Their Deity;"

ah, Vassula, see how My Father instructed you? rejoice then and be glad!

You left Your Royal Throne and Your Glory
to come to us Lord, assuming the condition of a
slave to serve us; no king was ever known to have
served his subordinates, and yet You, Eternal King,
King of kings came and served Your subordinates ....

You were made visible in the flesh
attested by the Spirit, seen by angels,
proclaimed to the pagans,
believed to the world taken up in glory ....
You came to ornament Your creation with a

prodigious Love that scandalized a multitude,
when You accepted the Cross,
leaving so many mouths open like gaping graves;
inebriated with Your Love for us,
You accepted to die and irrigate
Your flower-beds[170] with Your Blood,
in order to open Heaven and free
us from the bondage of sin;

Delight-of-the-Father,
Streams of faithful Love flowed from
Your Heart and in the folly of Your Love,
Lover of mankind, You accepted the
scandal of the Cross, and all its sufferings;

O Spring of the universe, perfuming the universe,
most lovable Bridegroom,
You are visiting once more the earth,
perfuming nation after nation,
but until when will those who roam on this
earth not notice Your perfume?

I am the Gateway through which the virtuous enter; not until they repent and make reparations will their nostrils open to inhale My sweet fragrance and revive; as for you, I want you as a lily, distilling purity, distilling myrrh on My Church to fragrance the House which I bought with My Own Blood through My Sacrifice on My Cross; remain near Me to spread your perfume all around; bear My Cross with tenderness and always remain enamoured of It ♡

have My Peace;   **ic**

---

[170] *souls*

6. 6. 2000

Scripture tells us not to have fear in
approaching the throne of grace to receive
mercy and to find grace when we
are in need of help;[171]

Now, from Heaven, You are showing,
and I would say, parading, Your
mercy on us, to transform our actual state
into a better state
that will lead us into the way of salvation;

the throne of grace decided,
the throne of grace disturbed
by accumulated sins, stepped out
and pronounced an order,

"We have said, 'blessed are the pure in heart,
for they shall see God',
today, this generation,
who feigns not to understand Us,
will never ever see Us and in their state,
will never reach their resting place;
how, in their actual state of sin,
will We ever make Our abode in them
and they in Us?
O devastated generation!

---

[171] *Heb. 4 : 16*

From Us alone will come salvation,
Our Infinite Mercy compels Us
to pour on this generation
increased and unmerited graces;
Our Mercy will save many of Our children
who unceasingly resist Our Love;

From the throne of grace they shall
receive mercy to attain the perfection
that is required to enter Heaven;

Through Our mercy We will raise souls,
but woe to those hearts that are so evil
that they should want to diminish or disbelieve
or calumniate Our mercy;
it is with Justice that they will be punished
for blaspheming on Our mercy!"

How is it that an endless and vile battle
is being performed against Your Mercy
by so many of Your House?
How is it that, knowing Scriptures,
they are not aware of the
interiour inspirations of Your Spirit?

How is it that they cannot recognize
the Three who bear witness in Heaven?[172]

You, my God,
in Your Supreme Love and Mercy,
decided to choose an incapable and weak creature,
appointing her to act, according to Your orders,

---

[172] *The Father, the Son and the Holy Spirit;*

commanding her to prophesy,
and that is to pass on Your Word;

She was taught to offer prayers,
entreaties, and sacrifice,
to win a hearing from You;
she was taught to offer her will;

I made, my Lord, every effort to present
myself before You as a proven worker
who has no need to be ashamed, but
who keeps the message of truth
on a straight path;

I was called by You and I responded;
I was called by You, and I acknowledged You;
I was called by You and I repented of my sins;
I was called by You and they accused me;

They accused me and still accuse me
because I answered You;

You have annointed me to witness,
but they raise their voice to drown
Your Voice;

My daughter, you have done loyal work through My Spirit, by helping My Church; you have been and still are at the service of My people; you have responded to My Call;

look Vassula, My Mercy is offered to all who appeal to the Bridegroom; My Justice today permits My Mercy to approach the dead,[173] whose stench has reached My nostrils, to resurrect them; this is done by Divine Mercy; but the saving Justice of Mercy says this to all:

do not allow your heart to dictate to you and tell you: "how is it possible that God speaks as much as that to this woman?" that is to bring down My Call of Mercy; in other words, it is to bring Me down; these people's behaviour is modelled on the way of thinking of this contemporary world; have you not read: "who has ever known the mind of the Lord? who has ever been His adviser? who has given anything to Him, so that His presents come only as a debt returned?" have you not understood how rich and fathomless are My Wisdom and My Knowledge? how can a mere creature dare raise his voice and declare that he has reached to the root of My decisions or My Ways, without condemning himself? therefore, My daughter, everything there is, comes from Me and is caused by Me and exists for Me ♡

yes Vassula, I have called you and you answered Me, so that you speak for Me; I have called you to parade, as you said, My Mercy so that through this Divine Call many sinners would feel compunction and will be induced to make peace with Me and repent; then when they see the way I am treating you, and how many graces I have been pouring on you, others too may be attracted by My Tenderness and decide to change their lives and commence to live a true life in Me, knowing that once they decide for Me, they too will taste My sweetness; their devotions will increase and those who lived without any devotions, will learn as well to pray without ceasing ....

---

[173] *spiritual dead*

today your Creator is telling you that in your silence I take My rest; in your amourous sighs for Me, your Lord and God, I receive garlands of perfumed glory; in your zeal for My House, I receive praise and My Body is soothed from My tormentors with the balm of your love; like a golden stream, beautiful to look at, I want to transform you for My Eyes, My beloved; I am your Creator and your Salvation;

no, I have stepped in you without any merit from you but I, when I saw you, I loved you; I decided not to deprive you of My graces but neither of My Cross; to lead you into the center of My Heart I had to diminish you, but I had neither lifted rod nor voice; I brought you to Me by My loving condescension;

hardly were you reborn when My Spirit brought you to cry out: "Abba!" overwhelmed with joy My Spirit together with Me and the Father blessed you thrice and immediately upon this, assembled the Courts of Heaven and said to them:

"We shall win great honour from Weakness; the Victory will be Ours in the end, but,[174] when news will reach those who harm the Church, they will wickedly advance against Our child; hordes of hard heartened people will demonstrate their evil hearts with savagery, but she will cleave on to Us and will be an evident sign to all of them that the Triune God is with her; and although at one time she would appear to them as the loser, in a short time they will realize that all their scheming was brought to naught;

---

[174] *As soon as this 'but' was pronounced, (it seemed that all the Angels and Saints understood before hearing the rest,) because of how it was pronounced they knew that sad news would follow; immediately their expression of their faces were grave and solemn.*

We will endow her spirit, for Our Salvific Plan, with courage and when she will speak for Us, she will speak with authority because she will be following Our Royal Command;

the officials in the beginning will take no notice of her and Our sayings; they will ignore Our Royal edicts, while Our Authority through her will be spreading out over every nation; and while Our Household will start renewing itself and being reborn through the Holy Spirit, the governor of the beast, the one who dares condemn Us, the one who treats noble hearts like criminals, will advance in massive strength against Our child and Our Noble Theme; but in reality his aim will be on Us;

realizing that Our Theme of Love endangers him[175] and his followers, since We would be revealing them and their long time plan against the Church, revealing to all the nations that they would force them and chain them to be fed, one day with naturalism and the other day with rationalism, forcing their law on them, wanting to subdue My Voice;

and as Scriptures say, so it will be done; Scriptures say:[176] "they will scatter the flesh of your devout and shed their blood all around Jerusalem, and no one to dig a grave!" because[177] "the beast that comes out of the Abyss", as Scripture says again, "is going to make war on them and overcome them and kill them;[178] their corpses will lie in the main street of the Great City known

---

[175] *He and his followers are those evil dark forces of our times who own the world and who combat Christ's Divinity and God the Father; they combat the Cross as well.*

[176] *1 Macc. 7 : 17*

[177] *Ap. 11 : 7 – 8; The evil forces*

[178] *Kill the mouthpieces who are sent by Christ & the Virgin Mary, in a symbolic way, by denying the fact that Mary & Jesus speak as two witnesses*

by the symbolic names Sodom and Egypt, in which their Lord was crucified;"

a well known populous city of Christ, known as the eternal city will never cease rejecting Our Calls, like Sodom's rejections, yet they will be claiming their openness and their openness to Our Spirit; but it will be the contrary, they will be crucifying all My given Words, nailing them to the wood;

at this, many priests will stand in tears before the altar, and while sobbing they will say: "Lord, do not let ruin come upon Your House; You have seen the vindictiveness of those[179] who have sworn to go against all Your Holy Rules and play the sages instead for, as they say, the well-being of humanity; these very jackals mock your Divinity, and they shoot venomous arrows on our faith; to fortify Your people and to fortify and warn your priests, You descended in Your glorious strength among us, appointing the winds as messengers and flames of fire as Your servants to bring glory to You; You chose them to bear Your Holy Name and parade It to bring honour to You by fortifying Your Household and reassemble Your flock, and to help Your House be called once more: One House of prayer; we give You thanks for Your Merciful Love and for having found a way of arousing us all from apathy;

but now, look how, when corpses litter Your city[180] and while the beast with its followers are trampling over them, rejoicing and celebrating over their death, look how they rejoice every time a negative judgment is pronounced by Your officials against Your chosen ones; so how much more will the Blood of Christ, who offered Himself, blameless as He was, to God through the Eternal

---

[179] *The evil forces*
[180] *from the Apostasy*

Spirit, purify our conscience from dead actions so that we can worship the Living God? how much more do Your officials need to understand that by rejecting Your interventions ever so merciful they are becoming collaborators, without them knowing it, with the governor of the beast and his followers?

Lord, most Merciful, You have found a means of warning all of us of the one who flaunts the claim that he is God; but now, look how they have stormed up against You to stop the mouths of those who praise You;

Our Lord and Heavenly King, come to our help! reveal Yourself with power in these times of great distress;"

a terrible oppression then will be put as a decree, although not a word will be in written form in the beginning; the holy ones and Our chosen souls will be constantly trampled underfoot and crushed, since through Our mouthpieces We reveal the schemes of the evil powers to warn Our people; We would be warning them from the beginning of Our Merciful Call that these evil powers who challenge Us, will be planning to alter the seasons and the Law;

then a time will come when Our Household will have no say over these powers of Satan and the dark forces, and still, they would not be understanding, even when they will be witnessing the sword raised against the Cross; the governor of the evil powers will be confiscating It from public places, and together with the beast and all his followers they will pursue their plan to dechristianize Our people, and still, Our officials will remain blind and will continue to ignore Our Merciful interventions, becoming associates with those who waged war on the Cross, without them knowing it;

then when they will realize that they had sinned, and that their constant debate of how it would be best to regulate and silence Our prophets was helping the enemy, they will confess: "Lord, we have sinned and done wrong, for we have betrayed Your teaching; we have not listened to Your messengers and only took them lightly; they spoke in Your Name to all people of the countries; saving Justice is Yours; but we have not listened ..." this is what We will hear;

you see, no matter how much Our child would be investigated and proven to be true, carrying all the signs that are needed and the blessings that come from above, the conspirators, with insolence, will pursue their evil designs;

over each nation they will have a governor and will be taking pleasure in their evil doings; but by her side, We will put a prince from Our Heavenly Courts, one of the highest ranked to be her guardian to help her detect the lying words and the perverted hearts; friends, rebels and sinners together will be called and revealed and Our golden stream will pour in their circles;

and We, in their center, will call each one of them by their name; "here is your Lord, your True Bridegroom coming with power; why, have you not heard that My Arm subdues all created things to Myself? should I deprive you now of My embraces on account of how you massacred My Body? or should I deprive you of My Merciful Love or My Goodness and not rouse you from your apathy? O no! My Love compels Me to save you as well and I will not deprive you of My embraces, nor would I deprive you of My sweetness, for had I, you would die;"

Our eternal and Holy Wisdom that is sweeter than honey will court their hearts so that their hearts may flow with the sweetness of Wisdom and declare:

"there is one God, one faith
and one Church!"

this will be in Our Ears like a melodious hymn; this will be Our Triumph;" this was what We said when We assembled the Royal Courts of Heaven;

be pleased to center your thoughts on Me and on My Divine interventions and you who say: "we do not need to see wonders", I tell you: "put your hand over your mouth and do not look at My Merciful intervention as an aggression, grant My people the grace to be saved through the wonders I am doing in your dark era; so do what is right and that is to walk humbly with Me, your God;"

My Vassula, learn that everything is under My Sceptre; come and contemplate My Saving Justice;

*How is it that they have not
believed or understood Your Language?*[181]

they have not understood the Bridegroom's language because I spoke in the terms of My Spirit and not in the terms learnt from human philosophy;

so My beloved one, have the mind I have and praise Me, rejoicing and do not listen to those who have not responded to My Hymn of Love; believe in Scriptures which say:

---

[181] *Rm 10 : 16*

142

"how beautiful are the feet of the messenger of good news ..."[182]

Scriptures never lie; be grafted in Me ....

ΙΧΘΥΣ ⊃<⊃

5. 8. 2000

I, Jesus Christ, bless you;

Lord, You who pulled me
from the mud of the mire,
showing compassion,
and who stooped from Your Royal Throne to me,
put a fresh song in my mouth;
I will proclaim and sing Your Word
to all races and nations;

do you want Me to sweeten My Banquet? the Banquet that I have been giving you through all these years? shall I grant, My beloved, more of My Sweetness to invigorate your love and relieve and heal you? healing itself comes from Wisdom ....

Ah yes!
Lord, take pity on this
ungrateful generation;
let them acknowledge You in their life;
let those[183] who heard and read Your message
be freed from their

---

[182] *Rm 10 : 15*
[183] *Some people*

lethargic spirit for they read
without understanding;
You have proved Yourself
Merciful and Patient to them;
let them acknowledge You as
the Godhead
who binds them in His Love;

Is it too much to ask
the Holy One who perfumes all
the universe with His Love,
to send new portents that
contain Your Sweetness?

Rouse them with fresh wonders
that are as sweet as honey;
let the forked tongue who persists
his persecution on me
but through me on You, be healed;

take pity on those who
call on Your Name day and night
yet live without charity ....

I satisfied you and others through My Divine Message with one
of My greatest and noblest Banquets; a prodigious prodigy I
prepared for your evil times, and I have granted you all to come
and taste it; to taste My Banquet is to taste Me, your God and
your Creator, so that you understand Me;

Ah! my Lord! Your Words are
mystical and hidden and many who
read You in Scriptures and in these messages
do not penetrate into their Knowledge,

for Knowledge of God they are;
they are illuminating our soul and
intellect and giving light within us,
yet, I know that there are those
who read without penetrating in the
wisdom of Your Words and they
appear as though sealed to them; and
yet, Your Words are
True Contemplation, Wisdom and Truth ....

whosoever listens to Me and not to his voice will penetrate into My Wisdom and My Words will flash in their soul like a mirror facing the sun; whosoever after having read My Words will decline and honour Me with generosity and love, the scales covering his eyes will fall and will **see Me** in My inaccessible glory; yes, for his eyes will see with full clarity what was invisible to him and inaccessible and kept only for the holy ones;

perhaps My language sounds incomprehensible to you, generation, but have I not once said that on the day your scales covering your eyes will fall, on that day you will know that I am in the Father, and you in Me and I in you; have I not said that he who has My commandments and keeps them, he it is who loves Me; and that anybody who loves Me will be loved by My Father, and I will love him and **show** Myself to him; yes! and you will see Me in My glory;

My fullness is lavishly poured out upon all of you and through My grace you become sons and daughters, heirs and heiresses of My Father as I am; you become with Me as Scripture say,[184] "a royal priesthood, a consecrated nation, to sing to God praises, who called you out of the darkness into His light;"

---

[184] *1 P 2 : 9*

I, the Bridegroom of the universe in all My Majesty will come to him who would have declined wholly and My Spirit of Love will envelop him to draw him in the Bosom of the most Holy Trinity; then, such a soul having received such an intensity of light will obtain all the hidden mysteries and Riches of Heaven and will begin while still here on earth, to live as he would be living in heaven, for he will have stepped in the Beatific Vision; in other words, that soul will have a foretaste of what the Beatific Vision is like and will complete this Vision to its fullness the moment he will enter heaven ....

have you heard the saying:[185] "all flesh is grass and its beauty like the wild flower's; the grass withers, the flower fades, but the Word of our Lord remains forever;" and this is why your life is derived from My Word, revitalizing you; flesh is flesh and flesh is frail, but My Word is everlasting and Life;

to maintain your soul alive I will ceaselessly be giving Myself to you more and more, manifesting Myself to you in power and grace while I will be expressing My Heart to you and showing you things that no eye has seen and no ear has heard, things beyond the knowledge of man, for what is knowledgable to men is not the Knowledge one acquires through My Holy Wisdom and that flows out from My Divinity;

now that you have tasted the goodness of your Lord, Vassula, what have you to say?

Your goodness My Lord acquitted me;
without a single merit, You have acquitted me;

---

[185] *Is. 40 : 6 - 8*

I have done it so that you would have faith and hope in Me, your God; and what else have I done to you?

You have asked me to offer You my will; then ....

then I poured My Love in you, to obtain love from you; it is on account of this I am speaking and repeating Myself to all of you;

you can obtain the entire Godhead within you, dearest ones, Who will teach you sacred mysteries, sublime and Holy Knowledge that comes from Wisdom, and as a tree, Knowledge will be the tree growing in you with Wisdom as its root; and from this tree the virtues will sprout;

you say, daughter, that many who read My Words do not penetrate their meaning because they find them mystical and sealed; now I have explained what you have to do to understand My Words; and in declining I will be the All of your soul, your life, your well-being, your inspiration, your goodwill, your hope, your love, your faith, your joy and your Bridegroom upon whom you could lean, and your resurrection;

My loved one then will be selected as one amongst others of My collaborators who will be ruling with Me; then you could say, "I am living a true life in God, because I am participating fully in the life of the Most Holy Trinity"; yes, indeed; and although I fill all things without being contained by their limits, I can still dwell well inside a limited soul and become knowable to men without losing My transcendence;

look at yourself, My Vassula, and tell Me: what is the sign of one's transformation?

I believe there are many signs;

you are right to say that there are many, but what is the most sublime sign of all?

> *From what Saint Paul says,*
> *it must be divine love in the being,*
> *which is infused by a constant inflow*
> *of Your own Love in that being,*
> *transforming thus that soul to*
> *progress into spiritual depths,*
> *leading it to grow in its love and*
> *become deified, god by participation;*

> *Your Love divinizes and*
> *Love transforms our so evil image into*
> *Your Divine Image ....*

yes! Scriptures say: "fix your gaze on Yahweh and your face will grow bright", which means, 'you will be transformed into Yahweh's likeness', having given one's self[186] to God, this most visible sign of transformation takes place; from thereon other signs follow; the sign of joy, of peace, of growing charity and that is how, through charity a soul can obtain the Knowledge of the Triune God; the soul being transformed will be like a lamp shining from within and without with divine love and the Knowledge of knowing and understanding God;

happy and freed from the world and its darkness, that soul will fly to Me, and remain in My Bosom;[187] aflame with love, inebriated by My Sweetness, this soul will fervently seek how to penetrate even deeper into the Most Holy Trinity; and I, the most delicate Bridegroom will keep drawing that soul closer to the Flames of

---

[186] *will*
[187] *Expression showing the intimacy*

Love of My Heart and immerse her in Us to repose in Us and be able to rule with Us;

how then can any soul refuse what I am offering? I had once said that everyone in Judgment Day will be judged according to the measure of the love they have had while on earth; what have you to say?

I would say:

> *"what quantities of good things*
> *You have in store for those who fear You,*
> *and bestow on those who make You their refuge,*
> *for all humanity to see ...." Ps 31 : 19*

and I will say to those who are still attached to the world, that if you decide for Me, sincerely, and intend to make peace with Me, when you call to Me and come and pray to Me, I shall listen to you; when you search for Me, you will find Me; I shall indeed let you find Me, and I will converse with you and you with Me for I have loved you with an everlasting Love, and so I still maintain My faithful Love for you;

so come, come and tear away the veil that separates you from Me; come and contemplate the Holy One who will give you eternal life;

28. 9. 2000

From Your Temple my Lord,
hear my voice and let me hear Yours;
let this generation open their ear to
hear Your Words that are
sweeter than honey, even than
honey that drips from the comb;
David said:

"Your servants are formed from Your Words ..."[188]

and so they are, for look! what have you all seen? what have you heard? an elite walking among the elite? a philosopher or a high ranked member of a theological academy? have you seen someone dressed in royal purple, wealth, and aquiring worldly knowledge? no? then you who went out to hear what did you hear? an authority given by men? oh no, for those who seat themselves and govern you, are not anointed with the oil of prophecy; then what did you hear all these years?

a heart? yes! that is what you came to see and hear; a heart formed from My Words, who defies the evil powers and the dominion of the Evil one, but that raises My Name in praise and glory, consoling the disheartened and the distressed, nourishing the starved with My Words; you came to hear a lenient heart formed by Me and from My Words; yes, My servants are formed from My Words, and to this day, I sit on My Throne commanding that city, inviting all the passers by:

---

[188] *Ps 19 : 11*

"who has decided to discipline his life in Me? who has made up his mind to be corrected and come and abide in Me? woe to faint hearts, woe to the listless heart, woe to the proud and stubborn heart, their weight of sin shall draw them down to hell! today again I come to you, generation, to form you from My Saving Words, and anoint you to do good; do not remain like a withered tree, come to Me and I will blossom you, and your fruit will be good; come to Me and when I will touch your lips, your lips will drip with kindness and you will be delivered from death ♡"

Yahweh guides our steps,
otherwise how can you on your
own see where you are going?
Yahweh's Throne can only be
mounted on kindness, Scriptures say it;

and so it is .... so do not say, "with whose authority has she[189] come to speak to us?" I am her Authority and this Authority has come to tell the mockers,[190] "I will expel you from your seats but I will lift the lowly to send them out and evangelize a dechristianized people;" I drew a long breath, sighing, while I was passing by those mockers; entirely overgrown is their spirit with nettles; as I was gazing on the Vineyard[191] My Son Jesus Christ left to them,[192] I drew another long breath; "where is the banquet of fine wines? of food rich and juicy, of fine strained wines? is this the place where a thousand vines used to be?

---

[189] *Apparently God means me ...*
[190] *God made me understand that He means the shepherds who behave like 'Cain' and do not pasture the sheep confided to them. They are those who are like wolves dressed in sheepskin; some of them have high positions, and persecute the 'Abels', the good and faithful shepherds and all His Good Works;*
[191] *Symbolic name for Church*
[192] *the Keepers, which means the priests*

"ah, generation, how I pity you! poverty is at your elbow and, like a beggar, want;[193] "eat honey,[194] since it is good; honey that drips from the comb is sweet to the taste and will save you!" says I; but nobody truly listens, only a remnant is eager to listen;

a House was built by Wisdom, bought by Precious Blood; suddenly the vengeance of Satan rose to destroy It; "whom shall I send to do this work of destruction? why, I will send the Beast and his followers to tear down and divide, to profane and abolish that which is most Holy ...."

when adversity came, I came to rescue, but no one truly, from the officials of the Church, listened; "it is only a private revelation, you need not lend your ear to it;" they would say;

to conceal My Voice is a mortal sin; to sift Me through and through and scan Me is an abhorrent sin in My Eyes; will your incredulity say one day: "but look, we did not know; we did not know that we offended Your Mercy;" indeed you have offended My Mercy; not only have you offended My Mercy but you have allowed the evil powers to gain ground and despoil the House My Son bought with His Precious Blood, because of your incredulity; and how! how ingeniously you get round My Words in order to justify your incredulity!

do you not realize that you have taken My Seat? do you realize that you are becoming the enemy of the whole human race? since hindering and diminishing the value of My Words through My prophets you are obstructing them from pronouncing My Will to My people and from gathering together and uniting the House of My Son?

---

[193] *Pr. 24 : 34*
[194] *Symbolic for God's Word*

have you not heard: "where there is no vision the people get out of hand; blessed are they who keep the Precept;"[195]

> *I am praying for this one*
> *who called out to you:*
> *"I have come to despair of all*
> *the efforts I have expended under the sun ...."*

and I tell him: "you have not toiled in vain; I have no pleasure in this division which is a grave sin, but unity is not beyond your reach"; many distorted words will come from many hearts, but am I not calling meanwhile? if you lose heart, turn to Me ....

"My servants are formed from My Words", My Spirit said to David; and you will recognize them in their speech and by what they utter; this generation is pining away, so will I not intervene in such an apostasy? the ravager is ravaging Our Vineyards, plundering the Scriptures and you know it; will I not intervene? look! My Abels are lamenting in the desert; My ambassadors of peace weep bitterly on the hardness of your heart as My Son wept bitterly over the hardness of heart, of Jerusalem, who persecuted every prophet ....

until when, Lord?

until they learn how to cry out:

"blessings on him who comes in the name of the Lord!"[196]

and as for you, Vassula, I tell you: I find My delight in you when you observe and do not forget My Words that formed you and

---

[195] *Pr 29 : 18 "Vision" is probably a prophetic gift; "the Precept" may be the prophet's teaching or else the Law ....*
[196] *Mt 23 : 39*

through you others; keep your eyes open to contemplate My inestimable treasures and My marvels of My Words; I have said, My Vassula, that contemplating the light of My Glory is above all theology; why, is there anything greater in the world than penetrating into your God and enjoying yourselves in His Presence? what is greater in the world than seeing Me, the Godhead? the One who is robed in Majesty and in Power is speaking to you; I transcend and reign in the heights of Glory, so that is where your eyes should be lifted permanently and you will be saved;

this is what you should keep teaching this generation; go and recite My deeds so that this generation opens its heart to Me and that I, in My turn, open the gates of virtue on it;

cry out to the shepherds guarding the Church and ask them: "has anybody out there tasted the sweetness and goodness of our Lord? is there anybody in there who excels in knowledge of God?"

if you say 'yes', for the first question and 'no' to My second question, then, why are you persecuting Me? I entreated and you condemned; I visited you shining My benevolence on you, but arrogance and hostility were your offerings to Me; I knocked at your door, but you did not open to Me and made sure your windows were barred as well; you made no room for your Lord; am I now to praise your discourse and your flow of words given to Me in My Assemblies? since all these words are empty with emptiness; what purpose do you serve? humble yourselves before you fall ill; let My Words be your educator, your counsellor and your delight;

and you   shall live ....

16. 10. 2000

The Lord is good
for He has taught me;
He is known to teach and instruct
the poor and the wretched;

My Father, your Father, is robed in Power
and Majesty; let us with one voice praise Him
and fulfil the vows you and I made
to the Most High;

Let us address our poem to the King;
but how I fear to hear:

"Have you been present at My Council?"

do not fear, I have driven you out of beneath the ground, I have unburied you, and said:

"peace will be yours, My child;"

out of the land of Egypt I brought forth prophets and saints; a blessing on the land of Egypt, may its foliage remain green and the trees that grow by the river Nile prosper and continue to produce their fruit to feed its people; a glorious throne was set in each place, where the Virgin Mary, My Mother, Joseph the Just and Myself passed by;

"Egypt, We tread on your soil and incense raised in heaven as we passed by; have you not read in Scriptures:

"Ambassadors will come from Egypt,"[197]

why, did you not know that I have anointed you as well?[198] no less than the height of heaven over earth is the greatness of My Love for you; may your soil continue to produce food and keep you cheerful;"

you asked, Vassula, whether I am fully in you, I the Transcendent God; I have, My beloved, displayed My signs and wonders in the one I favoured and have anointed you in My exuberant Love; inebriated by your weakness, I held you in My Hands, while Oil dripping like distilled myrrh dripped all over you, covering your head with drops of anointed myrrh, taking the shape of sapphires, in order to present you to the Father who, when seeing all the signs of His Son on you, would bless you[199] and would converse with you; in My extreme generosity I breathed on you My scent so that you spread its sweet smell around you, then, your enemies who are the dark forces guided by Lucifer and Satan and who are contradicting My Divinity will know that you have a Witness in

---

[197] *Ps. 68 : 31*

[198] *Our Lord made me understand that Egypt too, as the Holy Land, should be considered as Holy. Our Lord made me understand that Egypt protected the Holy Family when They had fled there. Egypt fed and gave drink to Them, but mainly protected Them and God never forgets a good gesture.*

[199] *It reminded me of Jacob's blessing Gn. 27*

Heaven and a Defender in the Heights that will uphold you until you accomplish your mission;

does all of this appear to you as extravagant? why, no one is equal to Me! I am not a mere scroll of a book! My Vassula, I am not just a printed matter! so much lack of confidence as though you had received thorns in your hands and not blessings![200]

let your enemies in their malice raise their threats at you, at Me, at My Divinity; let them; none of these will be allowed to triumph over you, none! and this is your God, the Most High speaking; let the sceptics, the rationalistic minded, the Pharisees of your time who to this day never tried to see Me in My Transcendent Light and My Glory, issue their knowledge and discernment from My Mouth, for I keep renewing My Creation .... but this is forgotten and I am as good as dead in their hearts;

I tell you:[201] "do not touch My anointed ones, do not harm My prophets[202]..." and to you, Vassula, you who fear that I ask you facing Me: "have you been present at My Council?" listen: did not Discernment give you light in your eyes? did not Wisdom whisper Her knowledge into your intellect all through these anointed years? on behalf of your nothingness and your wretchedness I, the Bridegroom, of My creation, leaned all the way to you, analphabet[203] child to My Word you were; uneducated and reckless to any flow of divine words you were, but nevertheless, beneath all this mire, screening you, I could see a noble spark for My Holy Name;

---

[200] *That day I was suddenly ravaged by doubts ... in my extreme weakness. The Lord patiently spoke to me as one speaking to a heart-broken child ....*
[201] *The Lord speaks to the sceptics*
[202] *Ps. 105 : 15*
[203] *Our Lord used the French word instead of the English one: 'illiterate', for it so pleased Him ....*

and now, to remind you: who reared you? was it not Wisdom? was She not your Educator? and who guided you to walk on sapphires[204] only? was it not Wisdom? and who enveloped you to soar up to the heavens? was it not Wisdom? have I not foretold you how I was to establish, through My Messages, My Kingdom in each heart? and that through My Holy Spirit I would discipline these hearts to turn them into apostles for your times?

child of My Sacred Heart, whom I intertwined in Me, "élla;[205] mi me fovásse, allá min amfivolíss ... se thiálexa yia to érgho mou ... affissé tis amfivolíes sou, élla ..."[206]

write: I will establish, as I said, My Kingdom in each heart that opens to My Word; do not fear of the abuses mortal men use to attack you, do not fear the oppressor's fury; I have sealed My Words on your heart and I have let drops of myrrh run on your lips so that they open with grace to herald peace and bring unity in the hearts of My sons and daughters; let the proud be astonished at your perseverance, which is given by My Spirit to those who are persecuted for My Sake, and let them avoid meeting you, as they do;[207] in My Day, I, in My turn will avoid them; while they deal with you harshly, lurking around you, bear this harshness humbly and with dignity, for through these haughty men you will receive your reward in heaven .... through your sufferings you are raising souls from their sleep or who have been carried away by the world;

---

[204] *Sapphires, represent the virtues here*
[205] *Greek*
[206] *Translation: come, do not fear Me, but do not doubt .... I have chosen you for My Work ... leave your doubts, come ....*
[207] *Some Bishops, when asked to meet me, as soon as they hear my name rouse to abolute frenzy;*

I will be revealing to you the furnace of My Heart; I will keep teaching you with the knowledge of Wisdom and will be blessing your steps while you walk with Me; as you walk in the path of unity, My bride, hold on fast to your Bridegroom and I will conquer in the end;

(God is near you and loves you! I Am)

(This passage is 'out of context'. Under the request of Fr. Gerhard Wenzel I opened this notebook on this page because he was filming from a distance. He wanted it to appear as if I was under dictation, when suddenly the Lord came and said, taking my hand, "God is near you and loves you! I Am;" The message above was not yet over but was left to continue;)

I am the Supreme High Priest over **all** My House, this House that men pitilessly divided in their lack of love; so, am I to keep seeing My House being divided and in such rebellion and not intervene? what are they[208] professing? in whose name are they professing their faith? I have cast down My Eyes not to see them while raising Me in their hands without faith, without holiness; yet, for the sake of My faithful ones, I descend in their hands; My Eucharist is given less and less importance;

I, the Illustrious King, Majesty above all majesties, Sovereign above all sovereigns, call you by grace to eat this time the living Manna, the Bread of Heaven, in form of the Eucharist; and so I tell those churches whose clergy have not accepted My Mystery: "come to your senses and seek Me earnestly, master your resentment, as well, against My Mother; may every race know that My Flesh and Blood comes from My Mother; yes, My Body

---

[208] *Those who have not yet understood that they will have to bend in humility and love to unite*

comes from the most Holy Virgin, from pure blood; blessed be Her Name!

to save all the humble of the earth who receive Me and to give them imperishable life I became Bread to give Myself to you; and through this Communion I sanctify all who receive Me, deifying them to become the flesh of My Flesh, the bones of My Bones; by partaking Me, I who am Divine, you and I become one single body, spiritually united; we become kin, for I can turn you into gods by participation; through My Divinity I deify men ....

have you not heard: "you too are gods, sons of the Most High, all of you;"[209] now I am judged by men; the Garment[210] that can cover you, adorning you majestically, giving you a metamorphosis, divinizing you, is rejected by those churches who cannot comprehend My Mystery ....

today again I cry out from Heaven: "brothers, why are you undermining My Divinity? if you claim that you are the ones who know what is right, then why is your spirit plundering My Church? I am inviting you to reign with Me, I am inviting you to rule with Me, I am inviting you to celebrate Mass and partake of the Divine Mystery in the manner I truly instituted;"

what if they do not listen?

the arrogant will endlessly jeer at Me, but this is because they have swerved from My Light; I am present in My Eucharist, but unless they see My Divinity with spiritual eyes, they will continue to be like a drowsing man, who, never grasps anything

---

[209] *Ps. 82 : 6*
[210] *Symbolic name for Christ*

you tell him; "what have you said? were you talking to me? eh?" he would ask;

kingly and glorious these churches proclaim Me, they affirm My might, proclaiming My fearful power, singing their praises to Me, acknowledging My Omnipotence and My mighty wonders, but I become a stumbling stone when it comes to measure the magnificence of My Divinity and of My Presence in the Eucharist ♡

today this is the stumbling stone rejected by the builders and they do not realize it is the keystone;

and you, My daughter, continue to proclaim Me as your only Love, and tell your brothers and sisters those words: "the Lord is good, for He has taught me; He is known to teach and instruct the poor and the wretched ..."

delicate girl I will share something with you: soon I shall let the dragon eat its own tail, I am soon to issue orders from heaven; I mean to restore My House; I will re-erect My Eucharist in the houses[211] that have been despoiled of My Presence and they shall become holy; you[212] have been pillaged from My Sovereignty, razed to the ground by the dragon, yet, I tell you, I tell all of you: My Spirit will be poured out on the earth to drench it with the dew of heaven and the grass of the earth will be greener, and the trees will bloom and their foliage will be beautiful and their fruit abundant, yes! abundant, wait and you shall see!

---

[211] *The Lord means churches*
[212] *The Lord means the church*

[213]"who tells you, you will last forever? you soared long enough like the eagle, setting your nest and sting among the stars;[214] now, come and face Me into battle; you will not be facing Abel; I will fling your dagger down; you have plundered My House, and you stole from within It what was most Precious; you have stolen to your heart's content; you have passed the gate of My people and you have blinded them; but now, your time is over, although you still believe you can extend your dark kingdom to mislead My people; no more of that; justice is ready to flow like water and My Spirit like an unfailing stream ...."

the time is near when one will cry out: "ah, the times are so good now ...." come, I shall give you rest to gain new strength; live My messages and follow the path I have traced out for you ....

ic

---

[213] *The Lord suddenly turned towards the evil one (the dragon) and said those words*
[214] *At the same time I heard "faithful"*

Epilogue

Does a work like this really need an epilogue? The words of this book speak for themselves. They need neither explanation nor intermediary. They are charming and simple. They speak to us of God and tell us that they are words of God. Words of God: another revelation?

There is only one Revelation of God, unique and definitive, and that is the Gospel of Christ. Everything that Jesus has taught us, everything that He did during His earthly life is engraved forever in the sacred memory of the Church. But the life of the Church is much richer and much deeper than what is readily apparent. It transcends the visible boundaries.

In this sense, the words of the Gospel of St. John that Vassula chanced upon are most meaningful: 'there are many other things that Jesus did: if one were to write them all, one by one, I do not think that the world itself would be enough to contain all the books that one could write' *(Jn 21 : 25)*.

The words and deeds of Jesus which the Evangelists and the Apostles were unable to put in their books remain in the Eternal Gospel. St. John writes in his Revelation: 'Then I saw another angel ... who flew to the middle of the sky, bearing the Eternal Gospel to announce it to those who live on earth ...' *(Rev 14 : 6)*.

This 'Eternal Gospel' belongs to the same Jesus who speaks to us in His Gospel. He has a heart-to-heart conversation with each one of us, those who have ears listen to Him. It is not a question of a different Gospel or a different Jesus for 'Jesus is the same yesterday and today, and He will be the same forever' *(Heb 13 : 8)*.

The whole history of the Church is full of accounts of personal revelation, mystical experiences and ineffable messages. For there have always been chosen men and women to whom Christ, His Holy Mother, or the Saints address themselves directly. But the case of Vassula is unique.

After being awakened one day by this personal revelation (her guardian angel spoke to her first teaching her about God), Vassula began to write down the words which Jesus Christ Himself spoke to her. Those words do not contradict the Holy Scripture and Tradition.

They should not be read as ordinary texts.[a] They should be read in interior silence. One must experience here the silence of eternity. It is a dialogue of a soul with its Lord, a dialogue that develops in the mystery of faith. This mystery is like the Light that illuminates the coming of each person into the world.

God expresses Himself in simple words: love, peace, joy. 'I love you, you belong to Me, you are Mine'. One grows in the understanding of these words that come to us from eternity. They must be listened to in the heart. They must be listened to in prayer. The words pronounced in this book have to become incarnate within us, they must take shape in us. They must become our dialogue, so that the prayer of Jesus becomes our prayer and the beating of our heart:

> 'Beloved Father,
> purify me by the Blood of Your Son.
> Father, purify me by the Body of Your Son,
> Beloved Father, drive away the evil spirit that is tempting
> me now. **Amen**

For this book of divine messages is a book of prayer: a single, uninterrupted prayer.

Vladimir Zielinski[b]

---

[a] *At the time of writing this for the first volume of 'True Life in God' in the original hand-written edition, Rev Zielinski was not aware that Jesus was later going to ask all readers of these messages to substitute Vassula's name with their own. The words, above, of Rev Zielinski sounded prophetic to Vassula when she first loooked at them.*
[b] *Rev Vladimir Zielinski is a Russian Orthodox priest*

164

Daily Prayers recommended by Jesus to Vassula[c]

Novena of Confidence to the Sacred Heart of Jesus

O Lord, Jesus Christ
To Your Most Sacred Heart,
I confide this intention ...

(Here mention your request)

Only look upon me
Then do what Your Heart inspires ...
Let Your Sacred Heart decide ...
I count on it ... I trust in It ...
I throw myself on Its mercy ...

Lord Jesus! You will not fail me.
Sacred Heart of Jesus, I trust in Thee.
Sacred Heart of Jesus, I believe in
Thy love for me.
Sacred Heart of Jesus, Thy Kingdom Come.

O Sacred Heart of Jesus, I have asked for
many favours, but I earnestly implore this
one. Take it, place it in Thy Sacred Heart.
When the Eternal Father sees it covered with
Thy Precious Blood. He will not refuse it.
It will no longer be my prayer but Thine, O Jesus.

O Sacred Heart of Jesus,
I place my trust in Thee.
Let me never be confounded. **Amen.**

---

[c] *In His message of 4 May, 1988 (Notebook 24), Jesus recommended
these prayers should be said daily*

The Memorare of St Bernard

Remember, O Most Gracious Virgin Mary
that never was it known that anyone
who fled to your potection, implored thy help
and sought thy intercession, was left unaided.

Inspired with this confidence, I fly unto thee,
O Virgin of virgins, my Mother!
to Thee I come, before Thee I stand, sinful and sorrowful,

O Mother of the Word Incarnate! despise not my petitions,
but in Thy mercy, hear and answer me.
Amen

Prayer to St Michael the Archangel

St Michael, the Archangel, defend us in the day of battle,
be our safeguard against the wickedness and snares of the
devil.

May God rebuke him, we humbly pray, and do thou,
O Prince of the Heavenly Host, by the Power of God,
cast into hell Satan and all the other evil spirits,
who prowl through the world seeking the ruin of souls.
Amen

24

deeper into the Most Holy Trinity; and I, the most delicate Bridegroom will keep drawing that soul closer to the Flames of love of My Heart and immerse her in Us to repose in Us and be able to rule with Us; how then can any soul refuse what I am offering? I had once said that everyone in Judgment Day, will be judged according to the measure of the love they have had while on earth; what have you to say?

25

I would say :

" what quantities of good things You
have in store for those who fear You,
and bestow on those who make You
their refuge, for all humanity to see "....

Ps 31:19

and I will say to those who are
still attached to the world, that if you
decide for Me, sincerely, and intend to make
peace with Me, when you call to Me and
come and pray to Me, I shall listen to you;
when you search for Me, you will find Me;
I shall indeed let you find Me, and I will
converse with you and you with Me for I

26

have loved you with an everlasting love, and
so I still maintain My faithful Love for
you; so come, come and tear away the
veil that separates you from Me; come
and contemplate the Holy One who will give
you eternal life;

A ☧ Ω

28. 9. 00

From Your Temple my Lord, hear my
voice and let me hear Yours; let this
generation open their ear to hear Your
Words that are sweeter than honey,
even than honey that drips from
the comb; David said:
"Your servants are formed from Your Words..."*
* Ps 19:11

27

and so they are, for look! what have you
all seen? what have you heard? an
elite walking among the elite? a philosopher
or a high ranked member of a theological
academy? have you seen someone dressed in
royal purple, wealth, and aquiring worldly
knowledge? no? then you who went
out to hear what did you hear? an authority given by men? oh no, for those who
seat themselves and govern you, are not anointed
with the oil of prophecy; then what did you
hear all these years? a heart? yes! that

Notes to the Reader

Punctuation

Punctuation in this book follows the original hand-written Messages where commas, semi-colons and colons are mostly used with the occasional full stop. Sentences begin with lower case letters except where the words refer to God or to St Mary (Our Lady) or where occasionally they have been used for emphasis. The spelling is also taken from the original Manuscript.

Vassula says: "I never understood why the text was punctuated in this manner until one day some priest told me that the Old Testament was written in the same style in Hebrew".

The Publishers have striven to replicate the hand-written messages in this type-scripted version, leaving spelling mistakes as they appear in the original.[d] That stated, they regret any error in transcription however minor.

Some pages of the original writings are reproduced on the pages immediately preceding these Readers' Notes.

Volume Numbering

This Volume XI (ΙΧθΥΣ) is the latest in a series of equally sized books prepared to replace the JMJ Series as stocks become depleted.

---

[d] *The reader is referred to the messages of 7.11.1989 (Notebook 38) and 25.2.1991 (Notebook 50)*

This new (ΙΧθΥΣ) typescripted series is also designed to be aligned (as far as practicable) with the 'Trinitas' Series of the Handwritten messages (Volumes I – XI).

For the avoidance of doubt the Messages in this Volume XI follow on directly from the Messages printed in JMJ Volume 7.

Headings

Headings are not shown in the main body of the text. There is, instead, a list of headings after the Introductions.

Biblical References

Old Testament

Genesis (Gn)

1 Maccabees (1M)

Psalms (Ps)

Proverbs (Pr)

Song of Songs (Sg)

Ecclesiasticus/Ben Sira (Si)

Index

Distributors (English Version)

Australia
Unitybooks
PO Box 228
Frenchs Forest
Australia
Tel: + 61 2 9975 4676
Fax: + 61 2 9975 4541
e-mail: unitybooks@bigpond.com

Marian Hampton Centre
261 Hampton St
Hampton Vic 3188
Tel: +61 3 9597 0333

Canada
Henri Lemay
Tel: +1 613 837.37.02
e-mail: henri.lemay1@sympatico.ca

India
Rev Stephen Raphael
St Ignatius Church
38 Ekbalpore Road
Calcutta 700 023 – India
Tel: +91 33 449 6641
e-mail: gasper@cal2.vsnl.net.in

Dr Celcio Dias
Tel/Fax +91 832 760600
e-mail: arvviegas@satyam.net.in

Francis S. Barretto
Strike Rich Investments
Athaide Mansion-B
Opp. Unitech City Centre,
Behind Mary Immaculate Chapel
M.G. Road, Panaji, Goa. 403 001
Tel: +91 832 230716/760077
e-mail: lionel@goa1.dot.net.in
        strikerich@im.eth.net

Ireland

JMJ Publications
1, Thornhill Malone
Belfast
Northern Ireland BT9 6RQ
Tel/Fax   +44 2890 381 596

TLIG Association
50 Kincora Drive
Clontarf
Dublin 3
Ireland
Tel: +353 1 833 9484 +353 044 66331 +353 1 2819662
Fax: +353 046-66399
e-mail: neasa@clubi.ie

Israel

Angele Lawrence
P.O. Box 17344
Jerusalem
Israel
Tel/Fax: +972 2 656 1519
e-mail: angele@netvision.net.il

Kenya
Linda Aquinas Agalochieng
P.O. Box 42654
Nairobi
Kenya
Tel: +254 2 444452/442154
Fax: +254 447459

Malawi
Gay Russell
True Life in God
P.O. Box 5423
Limbe
Malawi
e-mail: gayrussell@malawi.net

Netherlands
Stichting "Het Ware Leven in God"
Timorstraat 16
6524 KC Nijmegen
The Netherlands
Tel/Fax: +31 24 328 0067
e-mail: nl@tlig.org

New Zealand
Linda Owen
10 Smith Street
Waipukurau
New Zealand

Philippines

True Life in God Philippines Assoc
89 Scout Delgado Str
Diliman, Quezon City
Philippines
Tel: +632 374 3469
Fax: +632 372 3468
e-mail: tlig_phils@mail.com

Republic of South Africa

True Life in God in South Africa
37 Somerset Road
Kensington, Johannesburg 2094
Republic of South Africa
Tel/Fax: +27 11 614 3084
e-mail: tliginsa@hotmail.com

Evelyn Lebone
P.O. Box 830
Ladybrand 9745
Republic of South Africa
Tel: +266 310654
Fax: + 266 313085

Singapore

Wendy Yeo
275 Thomson Road, #01-10
Novena Ville
Singapore 307645
Tel/Fax: +2510311/2500063
e-mail: bnatural@singnet.com.sg

Switzerland

Tom Austin
PO Box
CH-1800 Vevey
Switzerland
Tel/Fax: +41 21 921 34 51
e-mail: tom.austin@span.ch

United Kingdom

English Association of True Life in God
PO Box 93
Wantage DO
OX12 8DQ
Tel: +44 1235 533990

Sacred Heart Distribution
PO Box 18
Cardigan
Wales SA43 3YH
Tel: +44 1239 615705
Fax: +44 1239 613192
e-mail: sacred.heart@virgin.net

True Life in God (Scotland)
Angela Parsons
17 Blinkbonny Road
Currie
Midlothian
Scotland
Tel: +44 131 449 5397

Distributors

Unity Publishing
PO Box 504
Bromham, Bedford
MK43 8SJ
Tel: +44 1234 825 937
Fax: +44 1234 825 779
e-mail: unity @tlig.org

JMJ Publications (See Ireland, above)

USA
Trinitas
PO Box 475
Independence, Missouri
USA 64051-0475
Tel: + 1 816 254 4489
Fax: + 1 816 254 1469
e-mail: american.assn.tlig@worldnet.att.net

Vineyard of True Life In God
609 Linden Avenue
Elmhurst, IL
USA 60126
Tel: +1 603 782 5882
e-mail: TheVinyrd@aol.com

101 Foundation Inc
PO Box 151
Asbury
New Jersey 08802-0151
Tel: +1 908 689 8792
Fax: +1 908 689 1957

International Website: www.tlig.org

Handwritten Version: Trinitas (see under USA above)